# BANNED

## QUESTIONS ABOUT THE BIBLE

Was Jesus ever wrong?

Did Jesus ever have sex?

Do Christians really think Jesus was white?

Do Christians have to be baptized?

Find your answers to these questions and more in the additional "Banned Questions" volumes.

*Banned Questions about Jesus*

*Banned Questions about Christians*

Are Mormons, Jehovah's Witnesses, Seventh Day Adventists, Spiritists, Christian Scientists etc., really Christians?

Can you be GLBTQ and be a Christian? A minister?

Do people have to choose to follow Jesus to go to heaven?

www.ChalicePress.com

# QUESTIONS ABOUT THE BIBLE

## CHRISTIAN PIATT

with Becky Garrison, Jason Boyett,
Jarrod McKenna, and others not
afraid of impertinent questions

CHALICE
PRESS
ST. LOUIS, MISSOURI

Bible quotations, unless otherwise noted, are from the *New Revised Standard Version Bible*, copyright 1989, Division of Christian Education of the National Council of the Churches of Christ in the United States of America. Used by permission. All rights reserved.

The opinions expressed in this work are those of the authors, and do not necessarily represent the opinions of the editors, the publisher, Chalice Press, Christian Board of Publication, or any associated persons or entities.

Cover image: iStockPhoto
Cover and interior design: Scribe Inc.

Visit www.chalicepress.com

10   9   8   7   6   5   4                    14   15   16   17

Print: 9780827202467   EPUB: 9780827202474   EPDF: 9780827202481


**Library of Congress Cataloging-in-Publication Data**

Banned questions about the Bible / edited by Christian Piatt.
   p. cm.
 ISBN 978-0-8272-0246-7
 1. Bible—Examinations, questions, etc. I. Piatt, Christian. II. Title.
BS612.B34 2011
  220—dc22                                                    2011005234

Printed in United States of America

# Contents

# Contents

# Contents

# Introduction

## Why a Book about Banned Questions?

When I was younger, I had a Bible thrown at my head for asking too many questions during a Sunday school class. Granted, I was probably even more provocative than your average adolescent, but I really did have a lot of legitimate questions about God, my faith, Jesus, and the Bible.

The message I got at the time was that church isn't the place for such questions.

Seriously? If we can't ask the tough, keep-you-awake-at-night questions within our faith communities, then what good are they?

I left organized religion behind for about ten years, until I found a place where my questions not only would be heard and tolerated but also would be respected and wrestled with. Beyond that, the good people at Chalice Press had either the nerve or the lack of judgment necessary to offer me a book series to help others struggling with these same questions.

In these pages you'll find fifty of the most provocative, challenging or otherwise taboo questions that many of us have wondered about but few have actually asked. I assembled an incredible team of respondents to offer their views on these hard questions. Their responses range from the personal to the profound and from sarcastic to deeply touching. I'm deeply grateful for each of them and for their commitment to sharing their hearts, minds, and experiences.

The goal of this book is not to resolve these difficult issues once and for all, but rather to open up an ongoing dialogue that allows us all to talk more openly together about what we believe and what we don't, and perhaps more importantly, why we believe it.

I strongly believe that any faith worth claiming should stand up to rigorous examination and should also be open to change over time. I hope that this collection is one step in your continuing journey as a person of faith, whatever that may look like to you.

If you enjoy this book, be sure to check out Banned Questions about Jesus, the second book in the Banned Questions series, due out in autumn, 2011. And if you have questions you'd like me to consider for future editions, or if you think of a topic for another Banned Questions book, write me at cpiatt@christianpiatt.com and tell me about it.

Christian

## Craig Detweiler

**Who is...**
**Craig Detweiler**

*I skipped second grade.*

Absolutely. Scientific principles have only been applied to the Bible for a couple hundred years. An earlier era understood divine inspiration as a different kind of truth. Shoehorning the Bible into scientific standards may actually reduce the profound gifts that the Bible provides. Shakespeare is not intended to be crammed into a test tube. Surely the Bible operates on an entirely different plane and claim to authority.

For example, we know that love is a powerful, elusive, but tangible reality. Artists and musicians have given us countless ways to describe such a profound truth. Drugs have enhanced the physical side of sexual performance. Yet medical breakthroughs cannot make us more loving. Becoming more loving is a lifelong quest, rooted in prayer, perseverance, and careful attention to others.

Following Jesus (the core Christian route) involves so much more than the minutiae of the Bible. We may memorize countless verses, but we are still called to put them into practice. Jesus seemed so interested in how our convictions turned into tangible differences for our communities. He gave little time or attention to those who tried to trap him into semantic arguments about obscure interpretations of the Torah. The Bible speaks into our hearts and minds with both veracity and variety. It is meant to woo, to persuade, to challenge, not by nailing down the details but pushing us toward applying timeless truths for today.

## Jason Boyett

Who is...
### Jason Boyett

*I can play the hammered dulcimer.*

Of course. Belief in the inerrancy of scripture—inerrancy is the theological word for the idea that the Bible is without error—is not a requirement for salvation. Let me be clear: A Christian is not someone who believes in the perfection of scripture. A Christian is someone who follows Jesus Christ.

Remember, the earliest Christians didn't even have the Bible as we know it. They had the Law and the Prophets on ancient scrolls. Certain churches had letters written by Paul. A few may have had the gospel accounts to read (and many certainly had other noncanonical gospels available, such as the gospel of Thomas). But they most likely wouldn't have made a big deal about whether or not these texts were free from chronological or scientific errors because they just didn't think that way.

The idea that the Bible's authority is tied to its lack of mistakes is an Enlightenment idea. In the grand arc of history, that's a pretty recent concept.

That's not to say the Bible isn't inspired or authoritative. It certainly is inspired in that it tells us the story of Jesus, from Genesis to Revelation. It is authoritative in that it is God's primary means of communicating with us. But the Bible is not part of the Trinity; to exalt it above the Christ whose story it tells, and whose salvation it reveals, is a bad idea.

## José F. Morales Jr.

Who is...
### José F. Morales Jr.

*I'm a techno/house DJ.*

Nowhere in the Bible does it say that one must believe in the Bible (let alone believe it's perfect) to be saved. Moreover, the Bible doesn't claim authority for itself within its pages. That's why I contend with my fellow Christians who say that one must believe in the "authority of the Bible." For me, the awesomeness of the Bible is that it points beyond itself.

3

And to what does it point?

First, the Bible points to the authority of God—not of the Bible! God is supreme above all, creator and sustainer of all life—life now and beyond the grave. I always say that the most important words in scripture are the first four: "In the beginning, God . . ."

Second, the Bible points to the good news of salvation. Now, salvation is defined in many different ways throughout scripture. So we should become familiar with the broad stroke with which the Bible paints salvation: God saves in creation, in gathering a community, in political liberation, in acquiring wisdom, in healing, and in the washing away of sin. In his book *Salvation*, Joel Green summarizes it best: Salvation is "God drawing near"—drawing near in creation, in the Temple, in Christ.

And we draw near to the Bible, the written word, because in doing so, the Living Word, whom Christians know as Jesus Christ, draws near to us (see Lk. 24:13–32). "They said to each other, 'Were not our hearts burning within us while he [Jesus] was talking to us on the road, while he was opening the scriptures to us?'" (Lk. 24:32).

God indeed has drawn near to save us—believe it!

## Nadia Bolz-Weber

**Who is...**
**Nadia Bolz-Weber**

*I have four chickens in my backyard.*

A World Religions professor of mine in seminary told a story about New Testament scholar John Dominic Crossan being asked what it takes to be a Christian. His answer? "If you're dipped, you're in." What Crossan was saying is that your baptism makes you Christian. And when we are baptized, it is in the name of the Father, and of the Son, and of the Holy Spirit.

Notice that we are not baptized in the name of the Bible. Why is this? Because the Bible is not the fourth person of the Trinity, even though it is often treated as such.

Again, this is where Lutherans get in trouble with some of our other Christian brothers and sisters. We believe that God claims us and names us as God's own in the waters of baptism. The action is from God toward us, not from us toward God.

For a really great treatment on the difference between viewing the Bible as Divine Reference Manual and viewing the Bible as Living Word, see *Making Sense of Scripture* by David J. Lose.

## Christian Piatt

**Who is...**
**Christian Piatt**

*I once had a job cleaning out condemned apartment buildings.*

There are two things to consider when dealing with this question: church history and human nature. One of the biggest reasons that Martin Luther resisted the authority of the Catholic Church the way he did, ultimately sparking the Protestant Reformation, was because he believed that people should not be beholden to the church in claiming what they believe about God.

So at the foundation of every non-Catholic Christian church is this value of the individual freedom of belief, at least in theory. But in reality, we humans aren't big fans of letting go of control, and church is certainly no exception. Although Baptists, Methodists, Lutherans, and all other Protestants supposedly have the liberty to interpret scripture without organized religion interceding and telling them what to think, we find plenty of examples where this still happens.

You know that old saying about those who don't learn from history being doomed to repeat it? For all the benefits of the church, we sometimes have selective amnesia when it comes to remembering where we came from.

Some religious leaders will say you can't be a Christian without claiming the perfect, inerrant authority of scripture. The good news is that you get to decide for yourself whether you agree with them or not.

## Joshua Toulouse

### Who is...
**Joshua Toulouse**

*I am currently pursuing my lifelong goal of spending the rest of my life in school. I really, really love school, and I hate the idea of living in the "real world."*

The Bible says that all scripture is inspired by God, or it can be translated as "breathed" or "spirited" by God. But nowhere do the scriptures claim to be handed down directly from God without possibility for error. While some traditions have understood scripture this way, it is certainly not a requirement for Christianity.

I choose to see the idea that scripture is inspired by God to mean that God inspired the writing of the scripture but also respected the humanity of those who were doing the writing. God recognizes that we are not perfect, and therefore nothing we create will be perfect either.

It is helpful to consider too that the inspiration of God regarding scripture doesn't end when the writing is complete. God is also inspiring those of us who hear or read scripture today. With this understanding, God is kept active in scripture, in that scripture can speak to us in new ways and on different levels now as opposed to when it was written.

The breathing or spiriting of God in scripture occurs today, just as much in our receiving of scripture as it was in the writing.

## Becky Garrison

### Who is...
**Becky Garrison**

*Since 1996, I've been studying improv theater with Gary Austin, founder of the Groundlings.*

This concept of reading the Bible line by line is a relatively new way of interpreting scripture that would have been totally foreign to pre-Enlightenment Christians. Even the most die-hard literalist acknowledges that when Jesus was speaking in parables, his audience knew that he was using metaphors and symbols.

To reduce the poetry, metaphor, symbolism, and other literary devices present in this holy book to a point where the Bible becomes a technical how-to manual misses the mystery behind the myriad ways that God has spoken to humanity throughout history.

## Jim L. Robinson

Of course! Christianity is not based on one's affirmation of scripture or the correctness of one's doctrine; rather, it's based on God's grace and our trust in that grace.

I don't buy the exact description of "inerrancy" that's such a crucial belief for some Christians. On the other hand, I believe that any perceived "errors" are not really in scripture but in human presuppositions about the texts.

The Bible is a human witness to the presence and grace of God. God interacts with humans and sometimes (by way of divine inspiration) some humans get it. They perceive and understand that presence and write down their experience. Down through history some of those writings have been collected to provide a standard by which succeeding generations can evaluate their own experiences.

As to "handed down directly from God," that's again a matter of definition. Yes, I believe that God is the source of the truth in scripture, but I don't believe that God dictated it word for word. The truth and the validity of the Christian witness are proven in the arena of history where God interacts with humans. We are known by the fruits we bear.

### Scriptural References

Matthew 7:24–29; 28:19; Mark 1:21–28; Luke 24:13–32; 2 Timothy 3:15–16; 2 Peter 1:20–21

### Suggested Additional Sources for Reading

- Paul J. Achtemeier, *Inspiration and Authority: Nature and Function of Christian Scripture* (Hendrickson, 1999).
- Karen Armstrong, *The Case for God* (Alfred A. Knopf, 2009).
- Marcus J. Borg, *The God We Never Knew: Beyond Dogmatic Religion to a More Authentic Contemporary Faith* (HarperOne, 1997), especially chap. 7, "Salvation: What on Earth Do We Mean?"
- Marcus J. Borg, *The Heart of Christianity: Rediscovering a Life of Faith* (HarperOne, 2003), especially chap. 3, "The Bible: The Heart of the Tradition."
- Ed Cyzewski, *Coffeehouse Theology* (NavPress, 2008).

- Bart D. Ehrman, *Jesus, Interrupted: Revealing the Hidden Contradictions in the Bible (and Why We Don't Know about Them)* (HarperOne, 2010).
- Bart D. Ehrman, *Misquoting Jesus: The Story behind Who Changed the Bible and Why* (HarperOne, 2007).
- Daniel Erlander, *Baptized, We Live: Lutheranism as a Way of Life* (Augsburg Fortress Press, 1995).
- Peter J. Gomes, *The Scandalous Gospel of Jesus: What's So Good about the Good News?* (HarperOne, 2007), especially "Introduction" and chap. 1, "We Start with the Bible."
- Joel B. Green, *Salvation* (Chalice Press 2003).
- N. T. Wright, *The Last Word: Scripture and the Authority of God—Getting beyond the Bible Wars* (HarperOne, 2006).

## Suggested Questions for Further Discussion/Thought

1. If you are saved by the Bible's lack of errors, what happens if you find a mistake in it?
2. How deep are you willing to go in Bible study? Are you willing to consider sources other than those that support what you already think you believe?
3. What kind of relationship should Christians have with the Bible?
4. Joel Green defines salvation as "God drawing near." How do you define salvation?
5. What makes someone Christian?

# Question

*If Adam and Eve were the first (and only) people on Earth, where did their kids' spouses come from? Did they marry each other? And if everyone on Earth but Noah's family was killed in a great flood, did Noah's kids sleep with each other? Isn't this a sin?*

## Christian Piatt

Stories like these are challenging for those who take the Bible literally because they lead to some potentially creepy conclusions. Consider, though, that people of this time and culture were story-tellers. Consider that they didn't have much hard science to explain the inner workings of the universe, but they did have parables.

There are two roots of the name "Adam"—one being "man" and the other being "earth," as in dirt. A common translation of the name "Eve" is "life." So while you can look at this story and say it's about two people named Adam and Eve, you can also think about it as a story about the beginning of "human life on Earth."

The story about Noah is an interesting one. It's also helpful here to think a little bit more broadly, recognizing that many cultures throughout history have yielded similar stories about floods and other catastrophes. Keep in mind, too, that folks back in those days didn't travel much, so their idea of what the world encompassed was pretty small. If a large area was flooded out, it might well seem to them as if the whole world—at least their world—was under water.

Like the story of Adam and Eve, the story of the flood and Noah's ark addresses the age-old questions of why bad things happen in the world and how we continue to endure them. This isn't to say that some form of inbreeding didn't take place back in those days. But considering the broader questions that these stories are meant to address helps to get us away from the little details we tend to get hung up on so often.

## Joshua Einsohn

### Who is...
#### Joshua Einsohn

*I don't mean to give any credence to astrology, but I do find it helpful when trying to understand someone's behavior . . . which I also find mildly embarrassing.*

This is the stuff that makes my brain explode when it's taken literally. The amount of tap dancing that is required to make these stories work exactly as they are told really confuses me. If the creation stories (note the plural there) were meant to be taken so literally, there would then be explanations of exactly how the fifth, sixth, and seventh humans came along. There would also be an explanation of why two creation stories are told at the beginning of Genesis.

If the flood story was to be taken literally, there would've been a verse thrown in about the very first lido deck and the accommodations made for the extra people so that Noah's kids didn't have to resort to incest.

The Bible does not answer all the questions it raises. Rather than bending over backward to try to come up with a literal rationale, why not assume that these stories were meant to teach, instruct, and give comfort? Just because Noah's family might not have been the only survivors on Earth doesn't make his story any less important.

In my physical sciences class in ninth grade, I made poor Mr. McCarthy insane by always asking why something worked the way it did. He would explain the physics behind it and then I'd follow it up with another: "But why?" Finally, I'd push him to his limit and he'd say: "Because God made it that way!" I asked if I could put that as the answer on the test and he was not amused.

Some things we have to take on faith because we can't understand them, but short of that, there is a logical explanation and we should strive to find it, even if the answer is: "It's a story to teach us a very valuable lesson."

## Scriptural References

Genesis 2; 6:5—10:32

## Suggested Additional Sources for Reading

- Marcus J. Borg, *Reading the Bible Again for the First Time: Taking the Bible Seriously but Not Literally* (Harper San Francisco, 2002).
- John Dominic Crossan, *The Dark Interval: Towards a Theology of Story* (Polebridge, 1988).

## Suggested Questions for Further Discussion/Thought

1. Do you think the stories in scripture are meant to be taken literally? Why or why not?
2. Can there be more than one interpretation of biblical stories? What are some different types of understanding you can think of (cultural, moral, historical, etc.)?
3. Jesus spoke often in parables. How did people react? Were they concerned with whether or not the stories he told were literally true?

*Aren't women treated poorly throughout the Bible? Why would any intelligent modern woman today even want to read the Bible?*

## Rebecca Bowman Woods

### Who is...
**Rebecca Bowman Woods**

*I was born in Alaska, but I despise cold weather.*

Growing up in the church, I learned the better-known stories of biblical women. By age ten or eleven, I had a few questions, such as: Why was Jacob allowed to marry both Rachel and Leah? Why was it such a big deal to be "barren"? Why didn't Jesus have any female disciples (or did he)? And was Eve really to blame for . . . everything?

By the time I discovered the really awful Old Testament stories and the New Testament texts commanding women to be silent in church, cover their heads, and obey their husbands, I wanted nothing to do with the Bible, or frankly, with Christianity.

What convinced me was reading about Jesus. Even though the gospel writers were male, it's clear that Jesus had an ethic of equality when it came to women. They supported his ministry and were among his closest friends. He rescued a woman caught in adultery from death by public stoning and then convinced her that her soul was worth saving, too. Some of his longest conversations in scripture were with women. When most of the disciples went into hiding on Good Friday, the women stayed by the cross, and women were the first to see the risen Jesus.

A closer look at the rest of the Bible shows a steady (if not sparse) line of women who played a role in God's unfolding story. Alongside the "good girls" whose names I learned in Sunday School are those who challenged the status quo, made the best of bad situations, and followed God's call to service, leadership, and ministry: Tamar, Deborah, Bathsheba, Esther, Mary Magdalene, Mary and Martha, Joanna, Lydia, and Priscilla. These and nameless others demonstrate resourcefulness, strength, and courage—all the more remarkable considering their place in ancient culture.

## Becky Garrison

While tradition tends to accord Mary with having found favored status with God (Lk. 1:26–38), let us not forget the women around Jesus who kicked some holy hiney. For example, Anna, the only woman designated a prophet in the New Testament, possessed the wisdom and foresight to see that this infant before her represented the Messiah (Lk. 2:36–38).

If Jesus truly wanted women stuck in the kitchen, he wouldn't have encouraged Mary to join the other disciples in their discussions. Instead, he would have encouraged her to hang back washing dishes (Lk. 10:38–42). Furthermore, when Jesus was told his family was looking for him, he replied, "Here are my mother and my brothers!" (Mk. 3:31–35). He would not have said "mother" had there not been females as part of his entourage.

All throughout his ministry, Jesus debunked the first-century Jewish tradition that treated women like property. His actions with the Samaritan woman at the well (Jn. 4:4–26), the woman about to be stoned for adultery (Jn. 8:1–12), and the female sinner who wanted to anoint his feet with oil (Lk. 7:36–50) marked him as a man who would break every holy law on the books so that women could be viewed as equals in the kingdom of God.

Let us also not forget that Jesus made his very first appearance as the risen Lord before a "lowly" woman (Mk. 16:9 and Jn. 20:11–18).

## Craig Detweiler

The ancient world was quite patriarchal. Women were rarely afforded the rights and equality we've all come to accept as natural and God-given. Plenty of examples of abuse are found in the Jewish scriptures. Eve is blamed for original sin. Women are rarely counted in ancient censuses. They are not given power, property, or even a voice. In a particularly haunting New Testament passage, the apostle Paul insists, "As in all the churches of the saints, women should be silent in the churches. For they are not permitted to speak, but should be subordinate, as the law also says. If there is anything they desire to know, let them ask their husbands at home. For it is shameful for a woman to speak in church" (1 Cor. 14:34–35).

So why read the Bible? Women may find themselves strangely moved by Jesus' relationship with the opposite sex. He goes out of his way to affirm the value of women who have seemingly been discarded by their culture. Jesus defends the woman caught in adultery. He pauses to refresh the woman at the well. He stops for a women suffering from an issue of blood. He heals Jairus' daughter. He responds to the cries of Mary and Martha by resurrecting their beloved Lazarus.

If women find themselves discouraged by the ghosts of a patriarchal past, they may find Jesus a surprisingly liberating figure. He upsets the status quo by addressing women, affirming women, and befriending women, regardless of their social status.

## Marcia Ford

### Who is...
#### Marcia Ford

*I hitchhiked from New Jersey to Texas and didn't get killed once.*

Many—but not all—ancient cultures were patriarchal societies in which men had all the power and women were treated as possessions. While there were exceptions throughout its history, most notably the elevation of Deborah to the position of judge, Israelite society perpetuated that structure. While some see the Bible as condoning masculine control, others interpret the biblical perpetuation of patriarchy as a way of working within existing cultural norms.

This background is what makes Jesus' attitude toward women so astonishing. Jesus healed, delivered, and saved women as well as men and never discouraged women from following him. There's evidence that the women who traveled with Jesus were largely responsible for underwriting his ministry. Women were treated as valuable human beings, every bit as worthwhile as men.

Those who see the Bible as misogynistic often interpret Paul's teachings limiting the role of women as representative of all of scripture. But they fail to realize how much responsibility women had in the early church and how much the male followers of Jesus—including Paul—relied on women to provide for their ministries and even correct those who misunderstood the gospel, as Priscilla did.

Intelligent women today have much to learn from the Bible once they grasp the stunning message Jesus brought to the women of his day. Never before had anyone, especially a religious leader, offered them the hope and promise of a new way of living that Jesus did.

## Scriptural References

Luke 1:26–38; 2:36–38; 7:36–50; 10:38–42; Mark 3:31–35; 16:9; John 4:4–26; 8:1–12; 20:11–18; Acts 2:17; 18:24–28; Joel 2:28–29; Galatians 3:28; Matthew 26:13; Judges 4:4; 5:7, 31

## Suggested Additional Sources for Reading

- Kenneth E. Bailey, *Jesus through Middle Eastern Eyes* (IVP Academic, 2008).
- John T. Bristow, *What Paul Really Said about Women: The Apostle's Liberating Views on Equality in Marriage, Leadership, and Love* (HarperOne, 1991).
- Christians for Biblical Equality: http://www.cbeinternational.org.
- Loren Cunningham, David Joel Hamilton, and Janice Rogers, *Why Not Women: A Biblical Study of Women in Missions, Ministry, and Leadership* (YWAM Publishers, 2000).
- J. Lee Grady, *10 Lies the Church Tells Women and 25 Tough Questions About Women and the Church* (Charisma House, 2006).
- Stanley J. Grenz and Denise Muir Kjesbo, *Women in the Church: A Biblical Theology of Women in Ministry* (IVP Academic, 1995).
- Liz Curtis Higgs, *Bad Girls of the Bible and What We Can Learn from Them* (WaterBrook, 1999).
- Craig S. Keener, *Paul, Women, and Wives: Marriage and Women's Ministry in the Letters of Paul* (Hendrickson, 1992).
- Virginia Stem Owen, *Daughters of Eve: Seeing Ourselves in Women of the Bible* (NavPress, 1995).
- Lisa Wolfe, *Uppity Women of the Bible* (Four DVD set, available at http://www.livingthequestions.com).

## Suggested Questions for Further Discussion/Thought

1. How do contemporary Christian women reclaim the legacies of Anna and Mary Magdalene?
2. How has your church used the Bible to either promote women in ministry or deny them participation in meaningful ministry?
3. Imagine being a first-century woman in Palestine who has only known a life dominated by men. What kind of impact do you think Jesus' teachings would have had on you?
4. Matthew 1:1–17, the genealogy of Jesus, includes four women: Tamar, Rahab, Ruth, and Bathsheba (called the wife of Uriah). Locate, read, and discuss these women's stories in the Old Testament. What do they have in common? Why do you think the gospel writer included them in the genealogy of Jesus?
5. Are women better off today than in ancient times?

*How can a God be all-loving yet allow people to be thrown into hell?*

## Jarrod McKenna

### Who is...
**Jarrod McKenna**

*I think Žižek's right in insisting that trivial "interesting facts" about the author function as a form of propaganda to show we are "balanced"; that is, "I'm not just a crazy activist; I also like Scrabble and long walks on the beach."*

The Bible doesn't say God is all-loving. In my work heading up an interfaith youth organization in Western Australia, I have often heard my Muslim friends speak of the ninety-nine beautiful names of Allah, including *Al Wadud*, "The Loving One." The Bible, however, makes a claim not just about an attribute of God but about the mysterious unknowable essence of the Holy Triune God—that God is not just loving, but that "God IS love" (1 Jn. 4:8).

The context of this verse is very important in responding to the question of hell. "Whoever does not love does not know God, for God is love." Jesus not only reveals God fully but also reveals what it is to be fully human. You don't need to be a historian to know that it's hell when we reject God by living like we were made in the image of something other than the Love revealed in Jesus (1 Jn. 4:9–12). Tolstoy wrote, "Where love is, God is also." It's equally true to say "Where Love is not—that's hell."

Any talk of hell must come in the narrative of the Creator who has acted decisively to redeem all of creation, uniting heaven and earth in the nonviolent Messiah Jesus. We were made by Love, in the image of Love, to participate in the dance that flows between the Holy Trinity that is Love and that we see fully revealed in Jesus to be Love, and this Love will one day cover the earth "as the waters cover the sea" (Isa. 11:9).

To not eternally be fully human by participating in the dance of Love that is God is . . . hell. Hell is what happens when we willingly decide to collaborate with the dehumanizing forces of violence, injustice, and misery that will be no more when love is "all in all" (1 Cor. 15:28). That is why C. S. Lewis could write, "Hell's gates are locked from the inside."

## Jim L. Robinson

**Who is...**
### Jim L. Robinson

*When I was nine or ten, a Sunday school teacher, frustrated with my incessant questioning, slapped me and reported my "disrespect" to my father, who inflicted great pain on my butt when we got home from church.*

One explanation is that people make their own choices and reap the consequences. The rules are clear and there are no excuses. Another response would suggest that "hell" is the extension of a primitive reward-and-punishment worldview that is not really consistent with later writings in the New Testament.

The bottom line is that none of us knows the mind of God. We walk by faith, not by sight. No matter what we conclude, there is no guarantee that we're "right." Unfortunately, there are those who spout teachings about grace but who still believe you have to "get it right" if you want to go to heaven. It's not grace if we have to do anything to get it.

Whatever I say is a statement of faith, not of knowledge. If we knew, there'd be no need for faith. Indeed, from one perspective, the opposite of faith is not doubt but knowledge; and if the New Testament is clear on anything, it is that we are justified by and through faith.

Personally, I prefer to err on the side of grace rather than rules, laws, and prerequisites. I find in scripture a movement away from law and toward grace.

I believe, projecting on the basis of that movement, that God does not "allow people to be thrown into hell." I'm relatively confident that present-day teachings about hell will one day be revealed as a human misinterpretation of scripture—either in the writing, in the reading, or in both. However, that is a statement of faith, not of knowledge.

### Scriptural References

Isaiah 11:9; 1 Corinthians 15:28; 1 John 4:8–12

### Suggested Additional Source for Reading

- N. T. Wright, *For All the Saints?* (Morehouse, 2004).

## Suggested Questions for Further Discussion/Thought

1. What is grace? Are there prerequisites to receiving grace? If there are prerequisites, is it really grace?
2. Can one "fall" from grace? How?
3. Do you believe in hell? What informs your understanding of it?

# Question

*What does "apocalypse" mean, and does the Bible predict one?*

## José F. Morales Jr.

"Apocalypse" literally means "the unveiling." Apocalyptic literature was commonly written during times of persecution. Revelation, for example, was written to an early church persecuted by the Roman Empire.

Revelation is commonly read as an end-time calendar. But that is not what it's for. The author tells us—twice!—why he wrote it: "Here is a call for the endurance and faith of the saints" (Rev. 13:10; 14:12). The author John wrote to encourage the faithful to persevere.

John encourages (and at times frightens) the faithful by "unveiling" the true reality of things. He reminded them, and us today, that the oppressive kingdoms of this world will not last. "With such violence Babylon the great city will be thrown down, and will be found no more" (Rev. 18:21). It encourages us by proclaiming that God, not evil ("the beast"), will have the last word. Christ will remain faithful to the end even if we haven't always been. "Faithful" is a common title for Jesus in Revelation.

As for "the end times," the Bible tells us many things. Yet there's not full agreement on the details. The overwhelming areas of agreement are two.

First, there will be a final judgment. Not nice to hear, I know, but good news isn't always nice. In *Surprised by Hope*, N. T. Wright asserts that judgment is when the wrongs will be made right. Call it prep for eternity! This may not feel good, but it is good.

Second, God will bring about a total renewing of all that is. "For I am about to create new heavens and a new earth; the former things shall not be remembered or come to mind" (Isa. 65:17; cf. Rev. 21:1).

Thank God we can endure until the end because Christ, as always, is faithful.

## Becky Garrison

Given I'm a satirist and not a scholar, I'd like to give a shout-out to the scholarship of Dr. Barbara Rossing, professor of New Testament at Lutheran School of Theology at Chicago. As Dr. Rossing reminded us, while the sensationalist and "nutty" *Left Behind* books have grabbed the media spotlight and made the bestseller lists, their depiction of the bloody and violent end-times differs from the way in which scholars throughout history have interpreted this book.

Rossing defines apocalypse as a "pulling back of the curtain" to expose the evils of the world. Using this logic, prophetic books such as Revelation serve as a wake-up call about what will transpire if humanity remains oblivious to the telltale signs from God that something is amiss in our world.

Rossing also reflects on imperial violence. Revelation affirms that the system of imperial violence will be destroyed so that a new kingdom can be ushered in where the lion can indeed lie down with the lamb.

## Jarrod McKenna

Two days ago, in front of a sea of blue cops, a woman who I had not worked with before came up to me and thanked me for facilitating a gathering of over 150 climate justice activists in a nonviolent direct action at a coal power station. She then remarked, "If only we as a society could move past that ridiculous legacy of Christianity that wants the end of the world." People around us smiled awkwardly and winced at the realization she didn't know she was speaking to one of the prominent Christians in the movement.

After everyone had a laugh, I had an opportunity to share my faith in Christ and affirm the very real danger she named—Christians who read the Bible in ways that feed sadistic fantasies for hell "on Earth," instead of heaven.

Like slam poetry, biblical apocalyptic language is "spectacularized" speech: a confrontational communication designed to wreck worldviews of listeners with words that open new realities describing time–space events infused with their theological significance. As N. T. Wright points out about Isaiah 13:10, instead of saying the empire of "'Babylon is going to fall, and this will be like a cosmic collapse,' Isaiah said, 'The sun will be dark at its rising, and the moon will not shed its light, and stars will fall from heaven.'"

This side of the resurrection, we can affirm in Christ the historical reality of Arundhati Roy's now-famous poetry: "Another world is not only possible, she is on her way. On a quiet day, I can hear her breathing."

## Jason Boyett

Here's the dictionary's answer: "Apocalypse" is the anglified pronunciation of the Greek word "apocalypsis," which is usually translated "revelation" and which literally means "lifting of the veil." The English word can have several meanings. Occasionally it is used as an alternate name for the New Testament book of Revelation. It can be a catch-all term describing a genre of prophetic Christian or Jewish writings from the centuries before and after Christ, for example, the apocalyptic passages in the book of Daniel. But most often, it is used to refer to some horrific future event—like the chaos and destruction described in Revelation.

Does the Bible really predict an apocalypse around the time of Christ's return? That totally depends on your view of apocalyptic prophecy. Many conservative theologians believe at least some of the bizarre events detailed in the book of Revelation are prophetic—that is, that they describe, in veiled language, something that will eventually occur. Others think these prophecies have already been fulfilled, most likely in the destruction of Jerusalem in 70 C.E. during the Jewish–Roman War (this, they say, explains the apparent immediacy of some of Christ's predictions, especially when he says "this generation will not pass away until these things have taken place" in Mt. 24:34). Still others explain apocalyptic literature not as prophecy but as encouragement for persecuted believers of that day and time, written in code.

The Bible's apocalyptic prophecy is so cryptic that I am suspicious of anyone who claims to have figured it out.

## Joshua Toulouse

"Apocalypse" literally means to show what is hidden, or to reveal. It does not have anything to do with an event that will end the world. The book of Revelation is an apocalyptic text that is also eschatological (a word that does refer to the end of the world), so for many, the word "apocalypse" has come to be understood as being eschatological, but in actuality, the word just means "to reveal."

The Bible doesn't predict, or even claim to predict, an apocalypse, although there are many times when it is apocalyptic in that it is revealing. The Bible doesn't really predict an eschatological cataclysmic event, either. While some people read Revelation in that sense, it would be more properly read as a metaphorical vision speaking to a specific situation occurring at the time of the writing.

The Bible can be read to say that at some point (and it doesn't give any real sense of when, considering it says "soon" and that was two thousand years ago) the present evil age will end and the age of the kingdom of heaven will be ushered in. As far as predictions go, however, the Bible isn't very clear on the specifics.

### Scriptural References

Isaiah 24—27; 65:17–25; Daniel; Matthew 24; 25:31–46; Revelation 2:8–11; 4:22; 21, 22

## Suggested Additional Sources for Reading

- Gene Boring, *Revelation. Interpretation: A Bible Commentary for Teaching and Preaching* (Westminster/John Knox Press, 1989).
- Gregory Boyd, *The Myth of a Christian Religion: Losing your Religion for the Beauty of a Revolution* (Zondervan, 2009).
- Jason Boyett, *Pocket Guide to the Apocalypse: The Official Field Manual for the End of the World* (Relevant Books, 2005).
- W. Howard-Brooks and A. Gwyther, *Unveiling Empire: Reading Revelation Then and Now* (Orbis Books, 1999).
- Lee C. Camp, *Mere Discipleship: Radical Christianity in a Rebellious World* (Brazos, 2008).
- Kenneth L. Gentry Jr., C. Marvin Pate, Stanley N. Gundry, and Sam Hamstra Jr., *Four Views on the Book of Revelation* (Zondervan, 1998).
- John Polkinghorne, *The God of Hope and the End of the World* (Yale Univ. Press, 2003).
- Barbara Rossing, *The Rapture Exposed: The Message of Hope in the Book of Revelation* (Westview Press, 2004).
- N. T. Wright, *The Challenge of Jesus: Rediscovering Who Jesus Was and Is* (InterVarsity Press, 1999).
- N. T. Wright, *Surprised by Hope: Rethinking Heaven, the Resurrection, and the Mission of the Church* (HarperOne, 2008).

## Suggested Questions for Further Discussion/Thought

1. If the word apocalypse means "pulling back the curtain," what do events like Hurricane Katrina, the war in Iraq, and global warming reveal for us?
2. Why are some Christians so caught up in trying to predict the rapture, the second coming, or other "apocalyptic" events?
3. What are we to make of Jesus' prediction that the disciples would see "the end of the age" come to pass in their lifetimes (Mt. 24) when it didn't?
4. When you hear the term "final judgment," what comes to mind? Do you believe there will be one? Why or why not?
5. How does our view of the end of things affect the way we live today?

## Christian Piatt

Perhaps nothing sparks more heated debate over scripture than the biblical position on homosexuality. First off, it should be pointed out that there is no reference whatsoever in any biblical scripture to homosexuality; rather, scripture refers in some instances to homosexual acts. Depending on your understanding of sexual orientation, there can be a big difference between the two.

The story of Sodom and Gomorrah is perhaps the most famous—or infamous—but it's important to understand how homosexual behavior was used in the town from which the term "sodomy" was coined. When a town was conquered, one way that the victorious army would demonstrate their dominance was to rape the women of the village. Sometimes, to add further insult to the defeat, they would even rape the men.

Rather than an intimate act, this behavior actually was a military strategy, though brutal and repulsive, to break the spirits of the defeated culture.

Other references, including those by the apostle Paul, condemn men for lying with men as if they are women. Again, some context helps us understand that certain non-Christian religions of the time conducted ritual orgies as a tribute to their god or gods, and though it can be argued either way, it's possible that Paul was referring to what he considered a heathenish religious practice rather than consensual gay sex.

Jesus never spoke about homosexuality or homosexual acts, so for those who look principally to him for guidance, we're left with our own consciences to guide us.

## Kathy Escobar

### Who is...
#### Kathy Escobar

*I hate wearing pants and socks, and I have lived in Colorado for thirteen years now. I'm the one in capri pants and flip-flops in December.*

The passages that are commonly used as an argument against homosexuality are Romans 1:26–27, 1 Corinthians 6:9–10, and Leviticus 18:22 and 20:13.

However, like all the translations of the Bible, there are many kinds of different meanings that can be drawn from the original words that people use to prove their divergent points. In the 1 Corinthians 6 passage, for example, which is often used, the word for "homosexual offenders"—*arsenokoitai*—has a wide range of interpretations.

That is one of the crazy parts about being more honest about Bible interpretation; it is subjective and always open for scrutiny if we respect our human limitations and inability to be 100 percent certain what God means. Regarding this issue, it is interesting that Jesus was never recorded in the gospels as mentioning homosexuality, yet clearly this has become one of the most significantly "Christian" issues of our time.

I come from a conservative evangelical tradition and have made great shifts in what I believe over the years as I began to realize that I primarily believed certain things because that was what people in power told me. As I started to do my own biblical research (and cultivate close relationships with gay and lesbian friends), my heart began to feel far less certain about what I had been taught. Because my church, The Refuge, is an inclusive community, sometimes people of a more conservative persuasion will ask me, "What we do about the gay people who are part of our community? Don't we tell them the truth about what the Bible says?"

My answer has become so clear and freeing. I tell them, "I know that you see the scriptures that way, and I understand there are some passages in the Bible that point to homosexual behavior as a sin, but it would be a good idea for you to know some other people who see those passages differently, who read the same exact words as you and have solid convictions—as solid as yours—that are completely different from your viewpoint. Maybe you can learn from each other in true community instead of arguing over the teaching of biblical truth."

Over time, I have come to the conclusion that I don't really know, but I don't really need to know. I don't have a simple way to reconcile these passages or dismiss created design and the differences between male and female anatomy. Regardless, I can say that all of the unknowns, various interpretations, and perspectives do force me to keep turning to and relying on the bigger story, and the bigger story is about Jesus alive and at work, restoring, rebuilding, healing, challenging, moving people of all shapes, sizes, colors, and sexual orientations.

## Joshua Einsohn

The Bible says a lot of pretty mean things about homosexuality: "You shall not lie with a male as with a woman; it is an abomination" (Lev. 18:22). (I know that the Lord was speaking with Moses here, but the subtle sexism should be noted . . . it overlooks woman-on-woman action.)

Leviticus goes back for more: "If a man lies with a male as with a woman, both of them have committed an abomination; they shall be put to death; their blood is upon them" (Lev. 20:13).

And lest we forget the New Testament, Romans 1:26–27 says that men and women who have homosexual relations are considered "unnatural" and pretty much have it comin' for their "perversion." Nice to see that women were acknowledged here, though. Progress of a sort, I suppose.

However, there are many laws that aren't followed today because they are considered antiquated or irrelevant. In Leviticus 19:20, it says that it's OK to doink a slave girl as long as she hasn't been freed and you feel pretty crappy about it afterwards. And there's also: "All who curse father or mother shall be put to death" (Lev. 20:9). I'm sure that the parents of many teenagers are game for that one, but modern law prohibits it and that's probably a good idea. We see very few stonings these days that aren't frowned upon, but it was quite the fad back then.

Many ancient laws, from keeping kosher to circumcision, are considered up for interpretation. Pro-gay-rights advocates claim that there have been mis-translations and inconsistent enforcement of laws. Many conservatives argue that these passages should be adhered to strictly.

All I know is that when I hear these words hurled at me and people that I care about, they hurt. A lot.

## Jason Boyett

The Bible explicitly condemns homosexuality, but these few passages leave room for interpretation. For example, Genesis 19—the destruction of Sodom and Gomorrah—is traditionally thought to have been a punishment on the cities' rampant homosexuality. After all, that's where we got the term "sodomites." But Ezekiel 16:49 says the sin of Sodom was arrogance, apathy, and neglect of the poor. So was God punishing Sodom for homosexuality in general? For something specific like rape or inhospitality? Or for something else?

Likewise, Leviticus 18:22 and 20:13 describe "[lying] with a male as one lies with a woman" as "an abomination." Seems pretty clear, right? But it also describes sex with a woman during her period as being an abomination. These verses are part of a holiness code to separate the Israelites from neighboring cultures. Some scholars suggest it doesn't condemn a homosexual lifestyle as much as it prohibits a specific pagan temple practice.

What about the New Testament? Romans 1:26–27 identifies homosexual activity as "degrading," but the passage seems to address ritual behavior or pagan orgies. First Corinthians 6:9–10 denies God's kingdom to "homosexual offenders," based on a confusing Greek word that probably refers to older customers of young male prostitutes (pederasty).

What's the point? The Bible condemns specific homosexual acts, but doesn't address what we typically think of as homosexuality today—homosexual orientation or loving, committed homosexual relationships. This doesn't mean the Bible approves of it but only that it is silent on the subject.

## Joshua Toulouse

There are two mentions in the book of Leviticus that say it is wrong for males to lie with males as if they were female, and these mentions sit alongside rules that say you cannot wear clothing made of two different materials. There are many laws in Leviticus that we don't feel apply to us now, and yet this one is still given credence by those that would condemn homosexuality.

In Corinthians and Timothy, two of the most cited examples of the Bible being against homosexuality, the real problem is one of translation. The word used is *arsenokoites*, which is only used in these two books. It has been translated in many places as either "homosexual" or "sodomite," and yet these are not clear translations for the word. Looking at the context, it is far more likely that these words have to do with sexual exploitation of some kind—either prostitution or rape—and not consensual sex.

In Romans, the issue is not homosexuality, but rather idolatry. Paul is pointing out to his readers the dangers of committing idolatry, and part of that is giving into lustful behavior. Paul looks at males lying with males and females lying with females as being outside of natural behavior, and therefore being solely driven by lust, because at the time there was no understanding of sexual orientation.

## José F. Morales Jr.

What does the Bible say about homosexuality as we understand it today—as an orientation, not simply as a choice? Nothing. Well, maybe something.

In the Levitical Code (Lev. 17–26), homosexuality is called an abomination, but so is eating shrimp and wearing mixed fabric. But we somehow don't get our cotton-blend panties in a bunch whenever we go to Red Lobster. We highlight one verse about "homosexuality" and ignore the rest, and have wrongfully used it to discriminate against homosexuals. Interestingly, most scholars admit that these verses are some of the hardest to translate and understand.

Then comes Paul. Paul reduces homosexuality to pederasty (men using boys) and cultic male prostitution. He had no concept of faithful, monogamous, same-sex relationships or of sexual orientation. Therefore, the Bible says nothing about homosexuality as we under . . .

But wait! Christian biologist Joan Roughgarden argues that we're looking in the wrong place. She says we need to see how the Bible treats eunuchs, for the term "eunuch" also referred to "effeminate" men, men with both sets of genitals, and men with same-sex attraction. This last one comes closest to contemporary understanding: "For some are eunuchs because they were born that way" (Mt. 19:12).

In the Law, eunuchs are condemned. But in Acts 8, a eunuch is baptized by Philip and portrayed in the text, and in later Ethiopian church tradition, as a righteous leader in the church.

And most powerfully, in Isaiah 56:4–5, 8,

"To the eunuchs who keep my sabbaths,
who choose the things that please me . . .
I will give, within my house and within my walls.
a monument and a name . . .
I will give them an everlasting name . . .
I will gather others to them besides those already gathered."

God is gathering the gays . . . awesome!

## Scriptural References

Genesis 19; Leviticus 18:22; 20:13; 19:20; 20:9; Ezekiel 16:49; Romans 1:26–27; 1
    Corinthians 6:9–10; Isaiah 56:1–8; Acts 8:26–40; 1 Timothy 1:10

## Suggested Additional Sources for Reading

- AllorNotAtAll: http://www.ALLorNotAtAll.org/resources.
- John Boswell, *Christianity, Social Tolerance, and Homosexuality: Gay People in Western Europe from the Beginning of the Christian Era to the Fourteenth Century* (Univ. of Chicago Press, 2008).
- Martin Copenhaver and Anthony Robinson, *Words for the Journey: Letters to Our Teenagers about Life and Faith* (Pilgrim Press, 2003), especially chap. 34, "Homosexuality."
- Evangelicals Concerned: http://www.ecwr.org.
- *For the Bible Tells Me So*, film, 99 minutes, VisionQuest/Atticus Group, 2007.
- Sally B. Geis and Donald E. Messer, *Caught in the Crossfire: Helping Christians Debate Homosexuality* (Abingdon Press, 1994).

- Peter J. Gomes, *The Good Book: Reading the Bible with Mind and Heart* (HarperOne, 2002), especially chap. 8, "The Bible and Homosexuality: The Last Prejudice."
- Daniel A. Helminiak, *What the Bible Really Says about Homosexuality: Explode the Myths, Heal the Church* (Westminster John Knox Press, 2009).
- Andrew P. Marin, *Love Is an Orientation: Elevating the Conversation with the Gay Community* (InterVarsity Press, 2009).
- Religious Tolerance: http://www.religioustolerance.org.
- Jack Barlett Rogers, *Jesus, the Bible, and Homosexuality* (Westminster John Knox Press, 2009).
- Joan Roughgarden, *Evolution and Christian Faith: Reflections of an Evolutionary Biologist* (Island Press, 2006), especially chap. 11, "Gender and Sexuality."
- Soulforce: http://www.soulforce.org.
- David K. Switzer, *Pastoral Care of Gays, Lesbians, and Their Families* (Augsburg Fortress, 1999).
- Mary Ann Tolbert, "A New Teaching with Authority: A Re-evaluation of the Authority of the Bible," The Progressive Christian Witness: http://www.progressivechristianwitness.org/pcw/pdf/Tolbert_NewTeaching.pdf.
- Mel White, *What the Bible Says—and Doesn't Say—about Homosexuality* (Soulforce, 2007).
- Garry Wills, *What Jesus Meant* (Penguin, 2006), especially chap. 2, "The Work Begins."

## Suggested Questions for Further Discussion/Thought

1. The Bible is much more forthright in its prohibitions against divorce; Jesus calls it "adultery" when divorced people remarry. Why, then, does homosexuality carry such a stigma in the church if divorce does not?
2. Read Romans 1:24–27. Paul was unaware of the notion of sexual orientation; therefore he speaks of "unnatural" homosexual relations. If we accept homosexuality, like heterosexuality, as orientation (i.e., as "natural"), does this change the way we interpret these verses? If so, how should we interpret this passage today?
3. In attempting to discuss the biblical view concerning homosexuality, what are the strengths and weaknesses of using the "eunuch" approach discussed earlier?
4. Do you know someone who is gay and a devoted Christian? What are you learning from them?
6. Do you believe homosexuality is a sin? Why or why not? What would it mean to let go of the need to be clear on this issue?
7. Do you believe homosexuality is genetic, environmental, or some combination of both? Explain.

What are the Apocrypha, the Gnostic Gospels, and the Dead Sea Scrolls, and why are they considered holy or sacred by some and not by others?

## Marcia Ford

The Apocrypha (from a Greek word meaning "hidden") is a series of about a dozen books that are considered canonical, or authentic, by Catholics and some Protestants but are omitted from some versions of the Bible. Even among those who consider the Apocrypha canonical, there is some dispute over which books should be included.

The gnostic (Greek for "knowledge") gospels refer to books about Jesus that did not make it into the canon of scripture. Interest in the books intensified in the last century with the discovery of a number of gnostic scrolls and in this century when books like *The Da Vinci Code* placed them in the spotlight once again. The gnostic gospels tend to question Jesus' humanity, suggesting that he was a divine or spiritual being who only seemed to be human.

The Dead Sea Scrolls are documents found in the mid-twentieth century that include portions of the Old Testament. Also found were apocryphal books and the writings of members of various Jewish sects.

As to the second part of the question, in large part their "sacredness" depends on what individuals choose to believe. Many Christians believe that because some early church leaders rejected apocryphal and gnostic books, we should too, given that those leaders lived much closer to the time of Christ, and for that reason their decisions can be trusted. Others believe that male leaders had questionable motives for rejecting gnostic books in particular, since they often presented a more powerful portrayal of women. The Dead Sea Scrolls present a different view of sects such as the Essenes than had previously been accepted.

## Brandon Gilvin

### Who is...
#### Brandon Gilvin

*I have been kicked out of Canada.*

"Apocrypha" means "hidden" or "obscure" and generally refers to books that are connected to the biblical tradition but were not considered sacred texts. There are apocryphal books in ancient

Jewish literature, such as The Apocalypse of Abraham, as well as in the Christian tradition, such as The Infancy Gospel of Thomas, which tells of Jesus' childhood misadventures. Although they may have had a religious purpose or have been "folklorish" complements to sacred texts, they have never been considered sacred.

Another set of literature is the "pseudepigrapha" or "deuterocanonical" texts. These are books that appear in Catholic, Eastern Orthodox, and Oriental Orthodox Bibles as part of their Old/First Testament but are not included in the Jewish Canon/Torah. They were included in the Septuagint, the Greek Translation of the Torah, which was used by the early Christian community. Protestants did not retain these books as part of their canon.

The Dead Sea Scrolls are a different set of documents. Discovered in the 1940s and 1950s at Qumran, near the Dead Sea, these documents include some of the only known copies of biblical documents made before 100 B.C.E. and give us much information about Judaism during the Second Temple period. Other documents are thought to be sacred texts of the Essenes, an ascetic Jewish community that practiced celibacy and ritual bathing. They are important because they tell us about a Jewish movement that is roughly contemporary with Jesus' life. Some scholars have even proposed that Jesus was an Essene, or at least practiced Judaism in a similar way.

The gnostic gospels generally refer to a set of literature found in 1945 in Nag Hammadi, Egypt. These thirteen scrolls—including the gospel of Thomas and the gospel of Mary, among others—are representative of Christian gnosticism. Gnosticism was a movement in the first centuries of the Common Era that held that the present world is an illusion and that through the attainment of secret knowledge (gnosis) we could break out of our illusory existence into something truer and more fulfilling.

These were excised from Christian communities as heretical, but are important because they tell us something about the diversity of Christian practice in the first few centuries C.E. It would be incredibly rare to find any contemporary Christian community that would hold the gnostic gospels as sacred texts. Though the popularity of *The Da Vinci Code* raised considerable interest in these documents, we know so little about their theological context and much of their meaning is so obscure, even to knowledgeable scholars, that their introduction into a religious community would be a complicated venture.

## Suggested Additional Sources for Reading

- Willis Barnstone and Marvin Meyer, eds., *The Gnostic Bible: Gnostic Texts of Mystical Wisdom from the Ancient and Medieval Worlds* (Shambhala, 2003).
- Bart D. Ehrman, *Lost Christianities: The Battles for Scripture and the Faiths We Never Knew* (Oxford Univ. Press, 2005).

- Craig A. Evans, *Fabricating Jesus: How Modern Scholars Distort the Gospels* (InterVarsity Press, 2008).
- Craig A. Evans, *Holman QuickSource Guide to the Dead Sea Scrolls* (Holman Reference, 2010).
- Joseph A. Fitzmyer, *The Impact of the Dead Sea Scrolls* (Paulist Press, 2009).
- Becky Garrison, *"Purpose Driven Heresy,"* a book review: http://killingthebuddha.com/ktblog/purpose-driven-heresy/.
- Wayne Jackson, "The Apocrypha: Inspired of God?" *Christian Courier*, September 21, 1999: http://www.christiancourier.com.
- Alister McGrath, *Heresy: A History of Defending the Truth* (HarperOne, 2009).
- Elaine Pagels, *The Gnostic Gospels* (Random House, 2004).
- Wesley Center Online: http://wesley.nnu.edu/biblical_studies/noncanon/index.htm.
- N. T. Wright, *Judas and the Gospel of Jesus: Have We Missed the Truth about Christianity?* (Baker Books, 2006).

## Suggested Questions for Further Discussion/Thought

1. How do we define heresy? What makes a work heretical?
2. How important is it that the early church fathers—with some exceptions—rejected the books of the Apocrypha and the gnostic writings?
3. Do you believe Christians should read the Apocrypha or the gnostic gospels? Why or why not?

# Doesn't the Bible condone slavery?

## Becky Garrison

The vast majority of us cannot comprehend growing up in a culture like first-century Judea where women are treated like property and accorded the same status as the family donkey. How threatening it must have been for patriarchal culture to be faced with such potential financial losses should their female property be set free.

No wonder Jesus was viewed as such a threat when he turned the entire social order upside down by blessing the very people vilified in first-century Judea and even invited them to have a seat at the feast in the kingdom of God. All were equal in the eyes of Christ.

Paul concurs with this assessment, encouraging Philemon to welcome back his runaway slave Onesimus as an equal, stating, "Perhaps this is the reason he was separated from you for a while, so that you might have him back forever, no longer as a slave but more than a slave, a beloved brother— especially to me but how much more to you, both in the flesh and in the Lord" (Philem. 15).

## Craig Detweiler

While the Bible contains timeless truths about the human condition, it also reflects its era. It was written during a time when slavery was an accepted part of the social landscape. Some people were enslaved due to political shifts, as when an army defeats a foe. They may have captured and enslaved the local people. Others may have been sold as part of the established economic order. Slavery was one way to pay off debts.

Into this unjust but established social context, the apostle Paul proposes a higher ethical standard. He challenges "owners" to treat their "slaves" with dignity. Paul even suggests that, within the Christian community, such stratifying categories should be ignored. While ancient cultures may have divided people into Jews and Gentiles, slaves and free people, in the Christian community all were to be considered and treated as equals (Gal. 3:28). That was a radical challenge to the status quo.

Unfortunately, over the centuries, many used Paul's discussion of how to be a "better owner" to justify slavery. Tragically, many Christians in the South held up select Bible verses to resist the abolitionist movement. White pastors (and slave owners) who refused to extend freedom and equality for all organized as the Southern Baptist Church. Perhaps the American Civil War could have been avoided if those biblical verses hadn't existed. But historically, the Bible has been (mis)used to justify many atrocities. Such historical mistakes demonstrate the ongoing need for thorough research and commitment to higher standards of biblical interpretation.

## Rebecca Bowman Woods

Unfortunately, the Bible has been used to justify slavery from ancient to modern times. One example is the "Curse of Ham," based on Genesis 9:20–27. Noah gets drunk and falls asleep in his tent, and Ham, one of Noah's sons, sees his father naked. Ham tells his two brothers, who go in and cover their father. When Noah finds out what happened, he curses Ham's son Canaan, condemning Canaan to eternal slavery in the service of Ham's brothers.

Originally interpreted as an explanation for the Hebrew conquest of Canaan, the story was later changed by clerics and others looking for religious support for enslaving black Africans. They argued that Ham, who inherited Africa in Genesis 10, was the one cursed by Noah, instead of Canaan. The name "Ham" was also mistranslated as "black" or "burnt." Legend developed that Ham's skin was darkened as part of the curse.

This story flourished during the transatlantic slave trade of the sixteenth and seventeenth centuries and was the major rationale for slavery in the antebellum-era United States, according to David M. Whitford, author of *The Curse of Ham in the Early Modern Era: The Bible and the Justifications for Slavery*.

Yet a study of the Bible finds no support for a link between slavery and skin color, as another scholar, David Goldenberg, pointed out in a 2003 interview with radio host Tavis Smiley. Moses had a Cushite (Ethiopian) wife, and "no one cared, and everybody was fine with it," Goldenberg said.

What can we learn from the Curse of Ham? The more familiar we are with the Bible and other religious texts, the more difficult it is for cultures and institutions to use holy scripture for unholy purposes.

## Jarrod McKenna

A preamble of context before my answer:

Am I not a man and brother?
Ought I not then to be free?
Sell me not to another.
Take not thus my liberty.
Christ, our Savior,
Died for me as well as thee.[1]

---

1. W. M. Swartly, *Slavery, Sabbath, War, and Women* (Scottdale, Pa.: Herald Press, 1983), 58.

These are the moving words and fine theology of ex-slave William Wells Brown. If we have ears to hear, they are also the words addressed to us by millions of people around the world.

Look at the label on the back of your shirt. Look at the shoes on your feet. Consider where you got that cup of coffee or chocolate bar. Unless God has opened our eyes to the suffering of today's slaves around the world (and as a result your community is actively seeking fair-trade alternatives), we are otherwise benefitting from a system that survives on the evil of slavery. It's important to confess and repent of the culture we live in *that does condone slavery*, and from which we have most likely benefited today.

When we read, "Masters, do the same to them [do God's will with enthusiasm and *obey* your slaves]. Stop threatening them" (Eph. 6:9), it's speaking to us. It's calling for us to have a relationship with those we are oppressing and obey them[!], letting that relationship transform us so that we no longer are oppressors and our sisters and brothers, are no longer slaves!

Paul has found a rabbinical loophole large enough to drive a kingdom revolution through the Empire's understanding of "order" without it being an instant death wish for all involved. It's subverting subordination by calling those who dominate into mutual submission for the liberation of both! Instead of "smashing the State" they are "subverting it" by being a living sustainable alternative, following Jesus in God's exodus from all oppression.

Desmond Tutu has said, "The Bible is like a knife. Some use it to butter bread to feed the hunger. Others use the knife to kill his brother." I think the challenge that slavery highlights for us is the way we read scripture. Do we read to justify the status quo that we benefit from? Or do we read the Bible through the story of Jesus as the fulfillment of God's liberating purposes through [ancient] Israel for all of creation?

If we choose the latter, we will find ourselves feeding, not killing; liberating, not enslaving. We will become God's nonviolent army of abolitionists for all who suffer, for all of creation.

## Scriptural References

Genesis 9:20–27; Matthew 5—7; Luke 14:15–24

## Suggested Additional Sources for Reading

- David Goldenberg, *The Curse of Ham: Race and Slavery in Early Judaism, Christianity, and Islam* (Princeton Univ. Press, 2005).
- Naomi Klein, *No Logo: Taking Aim at the Brand Bullies* (Vintage Canada, 2000).
- Brian J. Walsh and Sylvia C. Keesmaat, *Colossians Remixed: Subverting the Empire* (InterVarsity Press, 2004).

- Wayne Meeks, *The First Urban Christians: The Social World of the Apostle Paul* (Yale Univ. Press, 2006), especially chap. 9, "The Politics of Jesus" by John Howard Yoder.
- Mark A. Noll, *The Civil War as a Theological Crisis* (Univ. of North Carolina Press, 2004).
- E. Benjamin Skinner, *A Crime So Monstrous: Face-to-Face with Modern-Day Slavery* (Free Press, 2009).
- Stop the Traffik: http://www.stopthetraffik.org.
- Willard M. Swartley, *Slavery, Sabbath, War, and Women: Case Issues in Biblical Interpretation* (Herald Press, 1993).
- David M. Whitford, *The Curse of Ham in the Early Modern Era: The Bible and the Justifications for Slavery* (Ashgate, 2009).
- N. T. Wright, *Colossians and Philemon: An Introduction and Commentary* (IVP Academic, 2008).

## Suggested Questions for Further Discussion/Thought

1. Although slavery is illegal in many countries, there are more slaves today than at any other time in history, according to Benjamin Skinner, author of *A Crime So Monstrous: Face to Face with Modern-Day Slavery*. How do we define modern-day slavery? What are its forms? Why does it persist, and what can Christians do about it?
2. Do you think God cares about the equivalent amount of four jumbo jets of people (predominately women and children) that are kidnapped and "trafficked" each day?
3. What can you do in your daily life to help reduce or eliminate the oppression and enslavement of others?
4. Have you visited http://www.stopthetraffik.org and signed up?
5. What constitutes slavery? Which people in today's world do you understand to be enslaved?

*Was the book of Revelation written in code? Or had the author gone crazy? Was he hallucinating? Were the images portrayed to be taken literally?*

## Becky Garrison

I would try to explain all the various rapture-ready theories that have popped up over the years, but some of them are so farfetched I'd just laugh myself silly. I do, however, need to touch on what I would call "Darby's Dealie," because this seems to be the theory that is getting the most press attention.

For those who are not familiar with John Nelson Darby, this former Anglican priest and founder of the Plymouth Brethren propagated a new theology known as "dispensationalism," which introduced a brand new idea into evangelical theology: the rapture. Thanks to Darby, we have folks who have taken a metaphorical tale literally and thus translated metaphors into a code that they use as a lens to interpret geopolitical events such as the Holocaust, the Cold War, and the September 11 terrorist attacks.

Skim the Bible and you won't find the word "rapture," but you will find Darby's footprints all over the best-selling *Scofield Reference Bible* and the Left Behind series. What's truly troubling about Darby's teaching on dispensationalism is that it eliminates from the picture any talk of biblical teachings such as the Beatitudes. If you only focus on otherworldly things, then there is no point in working toward peace, social justice, the end of poverty and the like, on the basis that such projects are futile.

## Jarrod McKenna

The book of Revelation is not to be read literally but practically. John the Revelator is a guerrilla poet whose genre is Jewish apocalyptic, a potent political tool of resistance for the oppressed that he uses to seize our imagination in imitation of the Lamb whose nonviolence is victorious. John tells us to quit collaborating with the empire's gastric juices, destroying and dehumanizing life, because we are in the belly of the Beast. But by living God's victorious Calvary-shaped love we should give the system a stomach ache.

Despite the crazed rants of the radio preacher, trying to predict the end of the world with Revelation is like trying to use Bob Marley's lyrics as a street map. Not only do you get lost; you forget to dance. The dance of discipleship is one of the first things lost by those who long for the end of the world. St. John subverts Empire, the church, discipleship, and even our image of God with "the revelation": the nonviolent Messiah, Jesus.

We don't serve a God who is a Lion and a Lamb. The Lion *is* the Lamb! (Rev. 5:5, 6). Yes, there is a battle going on and we long for the Lion to be victorious! How? The Good Shepherd becomes a sheep and sacrifices himself like a slain lamb so that we can see clearly there is no more need to shed blood and, in the resurrection, opens to us a new world.

Unlike the radio preacher, we win not from world annihilation but from faithful nonviolent imitation (Rev. 12:11). We enlist in the "War of the Lamb" by dropping our weapons and taking up the cross of militant, nonviolent love. We are not saved from creation but from all domination. We don't go to heaven; by grace, heaven's coming here (Rev. 21–22).

Read Revelation through the person of Jesus, at the risk of ending this world of injustice and witnessing to the new world of peace.

## Jason Boyett

Most of the book of Revelation consists of a vision received by John, the author, while he was in exile on Patmos. The bizarre imagery of this vision does seem a bit like a crazy dream sequence, but it's worth approaching Revelation in light of its genre.

Just as 1 Chronicles is history and 1 Corinthians is an epistle or letter, the book of Revelation is apocalyptic literature. This type of writing—which includes parts of Ezekiel and Daniel and many nonbiblical texts—flourished from a few centuries before Christ until a couple of centuries after his death.

To explain Revelation as a weird hallucination—or for that matter, as a secret, end-of-the-world timeline for future events—is to ignore that apocalyptic literature had a very specific purpose. It was written to encourage believers to stand firm as they waited for God to restore the nation of Israel and defeat their enemies (i.e., Rome).

The symbols in Revelation, including the harlot, the beast, and the apocalyptic violence, probably refer to the Roman oppression under which its original audience lived. Though incomprehensible to us, the symbolism would have been clear to those first-century readers.

## Craig Detweiler

The book of Revelation represents an extreme style of writing known as apocalyptic literature. It is full of overstatements, hyperbole, and flights of fancy. It was written in a veiled way as a subversive form of communication. Apocalyptic literature was designed to provide encouragement for a persecuted people. In that sense, it was written in a form of code. Much of that code is undoubtedly lost upon modern readers. And it is a mistake to bring too much speculation to such a loaded book.

Looking back, we may wonder about the odd visions and references in Revelation. It is tough to recreate the figures and concerns of the early Christian community. Such evocative language is so far removed from our "realistic" appraisals of difficult situations. Revelation could be read as the hallucinations of a crazy man or as the enduring hope of a faith-fueled visionary.

The Revelation of John addressed specific concerns of its era. The encouragement to carry on would have bolstered those who faced persecution for their faith. They would have been buoyed by news of impending judgment upon their enemies. The lake of fire described in Revelation 19 would seem like appropriate punishment for those who tortured others. Revelation would have been read as a brilliant satire in its day.

Revelation also includes passages of poetic beauty. Revelation 21 and 22 envision a bright future, a heaven coming down to earth, and a radiant city that offers remarkable comfort. The description of the New Jerusalem rivals the splendor of an eye-popping Pixar film. It includes a river of life flowing down the middle of gold-plated streets, and magic trees with healing in their leaves. Like most great comedies, Revelation ends with a wedding banquet, where Jesus invites his extended family to dine with him.

## Scriptural References

Ezekiel 38—39; Daniel 7—12; Revelation 5:5, 6; 12:11; 21, 22

## Suggested Additional Sources for Reading

- Jason Boyett, *Pocket Guide to the Apocalypse: The Official Field Manual for the End of the World* (Relevant Books, 2005).
- Lee C. Camp, *Mere Discipleship: Radical Christianity in a Rebellious World* (Brazos, 2008).
- Stephen L. Cook, *The Apocalyptic Literature* (Abingdon Press, 2003).
- David Dark, *Everyday Apocalypse* (Brazos, 2002).
- Becky Garrison, *The New Atheist Crusaders and Their Unholy Grail: The Misguided Quest to Destroy Your Faith* (Thomas Nelson, 2008).
- Anthony Hoekema, *The Bible and the Future* (Eerdmans, 2004).
- "Understanding the Book of Revelation," PBS Frontline: http://www .pbs.org/wgbh/pages/frontline/shows/apocalypse.

## Suggested Questions for Further Discussion/Thought

1. What is the overall message of Revelation to you?
2. Why do Protestants and Catholics seldom preach on this book?
3. How can the violent imagery (e.g., Rev. 19) be read as a subversion of violence rather than support for it?
4. If Revelation was part of a larger genre of apocalyptic work, why was it declared canonical (part of the Bible) while other apocalyptic texts were not?

*Why haven't any new books been added to the Bible in almost two thousand years? Is there a chance any new books will ever be added? Why or why not?*

## Joshua Einsohn

**Who is...**
**Joshua Einsohn**

*I am angered and confused by (and stubbornly unaccepting of) willful ignorance.*

Considering the level of healthy skepticism and the wealth of knowledge that exists now that didn't exist two thousand years ago, it's highly unlikely that we'll be seeing any additions to the Bible.

We have science now and we can explain way too much for much of anything to seem like a miracle anymore. There's also way too much information out there; we can find out anything about anyone and at some point, we'd find out that a new potential prophet has a "nanny problem" or that they slept with a church member of the same sex or one of the myriad of reasons that previously reputable people are thrown under the proverbial bus.

Also, let's imagine for one minute that a well-respected member of society were to go up a mountain and come back down with new, crazy-sounding laws that they got from a shrub that was on fire.

Uh-huh.

Most of us would back away slowly and call the men with the pretty white jackets that have all those straps and buckles. Of the people who remained, a few would be potential believers. The rest would just want to know where they got the amazing weed.

The mystery and mythology of history has given the Bible it's "cred" and it would take a global communication crisis of apocalyptic proportions before that would change.

## Gary Peluso-Verdend

Who is...
### Gary Peluso-Verdend

*I was a very clean child.*

The early years of any religious movement are fluid. Over time, movements gel into institutions—or the movements and their purposes cease. The early gelling of Christianity included separating from Judaism (Christianity began as a Jewish reform movement) and distinguishing "orthodox" Christianity (right belief and practice) from heterodoxy or heresy. What became orthodox Christianity might also be understood as the victor in the battle against Montanists and Gnostics, to name two of the most prominent heterodox groups.

In the gelling process, the church developed creeds and a canon of scripture. Creeds, such as the Nicene, became a powerful measure of who was a heretic. The word "canon" means "measure" or "rule." Settling on a canon of scripture was one way the churches' teaching authorities tried to define authentic Christian belief and practice.

In modern times, scholars have subjected all truth claims to historical tests, including the claims of those who believed God led them to accept books as canonical. Even before the modern period, however, notable theologians disputed which books should be included in the canon. Martin Luther famously wrote that James is an epistle "stuffed with straw," and he did not believe that Revelation preached Christ.

I do not think the canon will ever be reopened. Once closed, a canon accumulates a history of usage that makes it more difficult than at the outset of the canon to add or delete a text. Also, in our present age, it is impossible to imagine an agreed-upon process, with agreed-upon representatives authorized to choose another writing that would be affirmed by all as word of God, report of the word of God, or reflection of the Word of God.

I cannot imagine such an effort producing anything other than headlines and grief.

## José F. Morales Jr.

### Who is...
**José F. Morales Jr.**

*I love sweet tea.*

Some believe that the Bible is closed, that no more books may be added. They base this argument on the warning in Revelation: "I warn everyone who hears the words of the prophecy of this book: If anyone adds to them, God will add to that person the plagues described in this book" (Rev. 22:18). Yet "this book" clearly refers to Revelation and not to the whole canon.

"Canon" refers to the standard collection of books accepted by "the church." Interestingly, to this day, the "canon" is contested within the church universal: Protestants, Catholics, Syriac Orthodox, and Chaldeans all have assembled ("canonized") slightly different collections. For example, the Church of the East (Chaldean) only accepts twenty-two books in the New Testament, whereas Protestants accept twenty-seven.

Nowhere within the Bible are there any specifications on what to include and how. And nowhere does the Bible "close" itself from addition. So we can feasibly say that books theoretically may be added. Shortly after the 1960s, some Christians in America and elsewhere considered canonizing "The Letter from Birmingham Jail" by Martin Luther King Jr. After all, it did have epistle-like qualities. Yet I think the consensus within the church is to leave it as is. (We're still trying to make sense of the books we have. Why add to the drama?)

This we can be sure of: We received these sacred texts, however assembled, as a gift from the ancients of our respective traditions—an imperfect yet wonderful gift to guide us in our journey. Our forebears collected these books because their hearts were stirred by the words in their pages and because they wished the same stirring upon the hearts of their children.

## Marcia Ford

### Who is...
#### Marcia Ford

*I'm a journalist who relies on phone interviews, but I hate talking on the phone.*

There are several reasons why new books have not been added to the Bible, the first and foremost of which is the prevailing belief that in the sixty-six books of the Bible, God has provided all that we need to know to believe in God and to guide our lives. A second reason is "the apostolic principle," that is, that the books of the New Testament must be related to the life or ministry of an apostle. This simply has not been possible since the second century. Based on the second reason alone, there would be no chance that new books would be added to the canon of scripture.

There's also the warning in Revelation 22:18–19, which applies to the book of Revelation but which many have expanded to apply to the entire Bible. It warns people not to add to or subtract from "the words of this book." But even many of those who apply those verses to just the book of Revelation would never presume to alter the Bible as a whole.

Remember, too, that there's no longer any central church authority that could make such a decision. As scattered as the early church was, Jesus' followers were nonetheless in communication with each other and with the bishops who essentially placed their stamp of approval on the books the churches were already using—books that now compose the New Testament. There is no such authority in place today.

## Joshua Toulouse

### Who is...
#### Joshua Toulouse

*I refuse to dance, not because I'm bad at it but because once I was dancing in the back of a moving pickup truck and got thrown out and dragged by said pickup truck.*

The process of finalizing the books in the Bible took hundreds of years and was by no means an overnight decision. But since the canon was ratified in the year 397 in Carthage, the matter has been closed. There are still differences among religious groups on exactly what is and is not canon, but there is no possibility of any new books being added. The books that are in the Bible were chosen because they were used consistently by many church communities and were largely universally considered as relevant and authoritative.

Although the canon was not ratified until the late fourth century, there were many proposals of a canon prior to that point. In most of them, the books mentioned as deserving of consideration as scripture are often very close, if not identical, to the books that we now view as the Bible. So even though there were some books that some groups felt should be included yet were not, and some books that groups felt shouldn't be included that were, for the most part the Bible we have now has been used for most of the last two thousand years.

Because of this shared history of communities viewing these books as scripture, nothing added now would have the same historical importance to the church as the books in the Bible. While other Christian writings can and do gain importance for various communities, recognition as actual scripture requires a tradition of acceptance throughout the history of the church as a component and that is something that no new book can have.

## Scriptural References

Jeremiah 31:32–34; Romans 15:4; 2 Timothy 3:14–17; Revelation 22:18–19

## Suggested Additional Sources for Reading

- Craig D. Allert, *A High View of Scripture? The Authority of the Bible and the Formation of the New Testament Canon* (Baker Academic, 2007).
- Karen Armstrong, *The Bible: A Biography* (Grove, 2008).
- Luke Timothy Johnson, *The Writings of the New Testament: An Interpretation* (Fortress Press, 2002), especially the epilogue.
- Lee Martin McDonald, *The Biblical Canon: Its Origin, Transmission, and Authority* (Hendrickson, 2007).
- Bruce M. Metzger and Michael D. Coogan, eds., *Oxford Guide to the Bible* (Oxford Univ. Press, 2004), especially "Canon" by Andrie B. du Toit.
- Jaroslav Pelikan, *Whose Bible Is It? A Short History of the Scriptures* (Penguin, 2005).

## Suggested Questions for Further Discussion/Thought

1. Do you think the Bible is open or closed for additions? Why?
2. If you believe the Bible is open, what criteria should be used to determine whether a book is "scripture worthy"?

3. Would a global holocaust allow room for new books in the Bible to be written? Would society be coherent enough to spread the new Word? Or would the total unraveling of communication that allowed for the emotional possibility of more books being written prevent those same documents from being disseminated?
4. Some readers of the gnostic gospels believe that such books as the gospel of Thomas, the gospel of Mary, and the Secret Book of James should be added to the New Testament. What do you think of this idea? Who would be responsible for making such a decision?
5. What books, if any, do you consider to be on a par with scripture?

*Is it true that the Ten Commandments found in the Bible are almost a copy of the Code of Hammurabi, which has been around longer? Why not just include the Code of Hammurabi instead of having a whole new set of rules?*

## David J. Lose

### Who is...
#### David J. Lose

*I own enough Norwegian sweaters to wear a different one every day of the week—and I'm not even a little bit Norwegian.*

A. The Old Testament contains two distinct kinds of laws. The first, absolute law, is binding in all circumstances—"You shall not murder" (Ex. 20:13). The second, case law, applies only to particular situations—"When an ox gores a man or a woman to death, the ox shall be stoned, and its flesh shall not be eaten; but the owner of the ox shall not be liable" (Ex. 21:28). (If you want to get fancy, the technical names for these are apodictic and casuistic law, respectively.)

Hammurabi's code is largely case law, written for specific circumstances; the Ten Commandments are absolute. While there is some similarity between Hammurabi's Code and the case law in the Old Testament, I'd argue that content isn't what makes Old Testament law distinct.

Instead, notice the small number of absolute laws that form what we might call the enduring heart of the law (ten commandments versus 282 rules from Hammurabi). All the other laws in the Old Testament reflect the ongoing attempt of Israel to apply the enduring and absolute law to their changing circumstances.

When we apply biblical law to our own lives, we will probably find little help from the context-specific laws. Instead, like the Israelites, we should faithfully discern how the heart of the law applies to our context.

Also, the Israelites ascribed the Ten Commandments to God, and by doing so portrayed God as deeply concerned with human welfare. This is a far cry from either the gods of Greek mythology—for whom human beings were little more than playthings—or the "Unmoved Mover" of ancient philosophy. Instead, Israel confesses that God cares about the way we treat each other, and so gave the Ten Commandments as a gift to help us get more out of life.

# Brandon Gilvin

The Ten Commandments appear twice in the Bible. Both times, they appear as part of longer legal codes, in Deuteronomy 5 and Exodus 20.

It's really not accurate to say that they are an exact copy of the Code of Hammurabi, an ancient legal code from Babylon (modern day Iraq). People who study the history of the Bible, however, do pay attention to the Code of Hammurabi, but because the Hammurabi Code clearly influenced the legal codes of ancient Israel.

Many of the laws themselves are similar, but more importantly, they exhibit an understanding that Prince Hammurabi offered legal protection to his citizens as long as they fulfilled the obligations expected of subjects.

Ancient Israelite legal codes are similar in the exchange of allegiance for protection. However, a good portion of Israel's history included a rejection of kingship as a way of remaining distinctive as a nation, so the legal contract in ancient Israel was directly between God and God's people. Whereas Hammurabi was conceptualized as the locus of power and lawmaking, for ancient Israel, the locus was God.

Kingship emerged later in Israel's history, and even then, it was bitterly debated, as one can find in 1 Samuel 8—9.

## Scriptural References

Exodus 20—31; Deuteronomy 5; 1 Samuel 8—9

## Suggested Additional Sources for Reading

- Charles F. Horne, *The Code of Hammurabi* (Forgotten Books, 2007).
- William Walter, *The Codes of Hammurabi and Moses: With Copious Comments, Index, and Bible References* (General Books LLC, 2010).

## Suggested Questions for Further Discussion/Thought

1. If it were proven that the Ten Commandments were derived from another source, would it make them less holy or important to you? Why?
2. How does Jesus' commandment to love God and neighbor fit in your mind with the Ten Commandments? Do we still need them?

*Did God write the Bible? If so, why didn't God simply create it miraculously, rather than using so many people over thousands of years to write it down?*

## Gary Peluso-Verdend

I once saw a cartoon that pictured God (depicted as a male) in the heavens with a megaphone. Tubes extended from the megaphone to the earth, where four men sat at typewriters reproducing at the keys the words they were hearing. The cartoonist was trying, positively, to express the claim that the four gospel writers were transmitting what they heard from God, word for word.

I think the Bible is an inspired text but not in the way portrayed in the cartoon.

From one of the opening stories in the Bible—Adam and Eve—we learn that God chooses to work through and with human agents. One could argue that God could care directly for widows and orphans, feed the hungry, and house the sojourner. Instead, God chooses to work through us.

So it is with the scriptures. I believe God inspired persons and communities over the nearly two thousand years of history contained in the Bible. They were inspired with ideas and stories, with laws and morals and values, and with an understanding of a God whose character is love and who has created humankind to reflect the divine character.

When writers recorded the pieces that other writers and scribes stitched together over time into what today is our Bible, they included the words of God, the hopes and dreams and anger of their own communities, their insights, and both their cultural biases and their wounds.

What we have in the Bible is a community of interpreters of the word of God. It is exciting and challenging, in our day as in any day, to join that community and to dare our interpretations.

## José F. Morales Jr.

Short answer: No. God did inspire it, but did not write it (2 Tim. 3:16).

God used peoples and communities over time to give birth and breath to what we now call "the Bible." Before the written word was the spoken word, that is, oral stories and traditions that were transmitted within Israel and the early church. Israel understood its holy identity through these oral traditions: stories of creation and election (Genesis), of liberation (Exodus) and instruction (the Law), and of adoration (Psalms) and proclamation (the prophets).

These stories and some new ones shaped the early church: incarnation (the gospels) and mission (Acts and the epistles). So the Bible is a collection of the people's encounter with a God who creates, redeems, judges, and restores.

The oral stories were not committed to writing until something terrible happened. The Jews were deported to Babylon, and the Temple destroyed. These displaced and distraught exiles needed somewhere new around which to gather, being that they no longer had the Temple.

Over time, observance of "the Law and the Prophets" became a way to recreate a "temple" of sorts. And by writing it down, this "temple" of oral tradition was given concrete permanence. The gospels came about in a similar way, but within a shorter time span.

Christians adopted this notion of the "temple" being whenever and wherever the faithful gathered around the word. And they did this because whenever they engaged the written word, they sensed that they were encountering the Living Word, Jesus. "For where two or three are gathered in my name, I am there among them" (Mt. 18:20).

The Bible shapes us because its stories are our stories and because we encounter Jesus along the way.

## Kathy Escobar

### Who is...
### Kathy Escobar

*I am a distant but direct cousin of Abraham Lincoln.*

I believe God used people to write the Bible. Through divine inspiration, the words were recorded. At the same time, I do not believe they appear in the many translations of the Bible that I have on my bookshelf in the exact way they were originally. I think pastors and leaders must become more honest about that.

Translation always leaves room for human error, and despite that possibility, it doesn't affect my extremely high view of the transforming power of the Bible. I love how God can use the flawed to reveal the perfect. I have absolutely no idea why God didn't just magically make the words appear in a neat and tidy package, but my guess is that even if God had done it that way, the same things would be up for grabs when it comes to interpretation and haggling over what it means and says.

Using a diverse mix of people from a wide variety of backgrounds over a long period of time seems to be more God's style.

The quick, simple, homogenous way we long for is extremely inconsistent with most honest issues of faith. God's obsession with using "people" is fairly apparent, so it makes sense to me that the story would be told through them. And it would leave us with holes that only faith, as described in Hebrews 11, could fill.

## Joshua Toulouse

We are told in the Bible that all scripture is from God. It is usually translated as "inspired" by God, but the literal translation is "breathed" or "spirited" by God. However you translate the word, it doesn't say that God wrote the Bible.

Still, it is clear that we are to believe that God had an active role in the creation of the Bible. So even if God didn't literally write the Bible, the question is still valid: Why was it written by so many people over thousands of years?

While the Bible is bound for us in the modern era as one book, each of the writings in their original context was written for specific reasons and to meet specific needs. They were chosen as canonical scripture because they were seen to serve more than their original function. The writings spoke to believers in other contexts and in other times and continued to be used liturgically in worship or for teaching. But first and foremost, they served a particular need that would not have been met if the Bible had been handed down complete from heaven, written by God.

While these writings were meant for a specific time in a particular situation, the active participation of God, through breath/spirit/inspiration, has made them applicable to the religious community beyond that specific time or those particular situations.

## Jim L. Robinson

I know of no credible person or source that would say God "wrote" the Bible. A much more common description of the origin of scripture focuses on the word "inspired." A common understanding of inspiration might be characterized as an angel perching on Paul's shoulder dictating directly into Paul's ear the words of his epistle to the Philippians. Some understandings basically remove all traces of human influence or participation in the writing of scripture.

I believe the Bible is divinely inspired. I do not define inspired as "verbally, one-word-at-a-time dictated." In my understanding, God inspires (breathes into) a person or a community an acute and accurate understanding of the meaning of God's intention in any event or occasion. My reading of scripture is more concerned with overall meaning than with verbal accuracy.

Divine inspiration does not bypass human vocabulary and thought patterns. Truth is truth, no matter what the medium may be. Its communication is concerned as much about what is heard as what is said. In other words, if I say something that you don't understand, then there is no value in my saying it.

In order to be effective in communication, God conveys meaning to people and communities in their language and cultural contexts. They, in turn, communicate that meaning in their own language and contexts.

It is impossible to communicate the fullness of God in human language. God surpasses all attempts at human description. It often becomes necessary to use metaphor and hyperbole in communicating the understandings that God inspires. The Bible is full of the same.

## Scriptural References

Luke 1:1–4; John 20:30; 2 Timothy 3:16; Hebrews 11

## Suggested Additional Sources for Reading

- Marc Zvi Brettler, "Torah: Introduction," in *The Jewish Study Bible* (Oxford Univ. Press, 2004).
- *The Cambridge History of the Bible,* 3 volumes (Cambridge Univ. Press, 1975).
- Lee Martin McDonald, *The Biblical Canon: Its Origin, Transmission, and Authority* (Hendrickson, 2007).
- F. E. Peters, *The Voice, the Word, the Books: The Sacred Scripture of the Jews, Christians, and Muslims* (Princeton Univ. Press, 2007).
- Mark Allen Powell, *Fortress Introduction to the Gospels* (Fortress Press, 1998).

## Suggested Questions for Further Discussion/Thought

1. Is there a difference between "truth" and "fact"? Can truth be transmitted through a medium that is not necessarily fact?
2. Read Luke 1:1–4 and John 20:30. Discuss how these passages point to oral traditions that existed before any writing of the gospels occurred.
3. What are your thoughts and feelings about the "infallibility" of the Bible? How have your thoughts about that shifted or stayed the same over time?
4. Do you think that the words that you read in your particular translation are exactly what God said?

## Do Christians need to read the Old Testament? Why?

### Rebecca Bowman Woods

**Who is...**
**Rebecca Bowman Woods**

*I love most sports, including ice hockey and NASCAR.*

Would you pick up a novel, start reading in the middle, and expect to know what's going on? No, but unfortunately, Christians sometimes do this with the Bible.

The Bible's two sections form a continuous tapestry of narratives and perspectives, speaking of God's activity from creation through the end of time. Yet we can fall prey to believing that while the Old Testament has a few interesting characters like Moses, David, and Jonah, most of it contains stories of a wrathful God, outdated rules, and boring genealogies.

We'll take the Ten Commandments and Psalm 23, but who needs those half-crazy prophets and kings whose names we can't even pronounce?

If we disregard the Old Testament, we limit our understanding of both Jesus and the New Testament. Take Jesus' last words from the cross in Mark's gospel: "My God, My God, why have you forsaken me?" These words were first uttered by the author of Psalm 22 and are part of a Jewish tradition of lamenting—crying out to God in godforsaken times.

Sometimes Christians look to the words and actions of Jesus to justify ignoring the Old Testament. After all, didn't he sum up all the commandments as "Love God and love your neighbor"? Jesus healed on the Sabbath, socialized with people who were considered impure by religious standards, and made a ruckus in the temple.

It becomes easy to think Jesus was rejecting Judaism instead of opposing legalism and corruption by small groups of officials. From there, it's not a big step to disrespecting and rejecting the Jewish people today. Historically, we have seen where this can lead humanity.

## Gary Peluso-Verdend

Absolutely! This question was raised as early as the second century by a Christian named Marcion, who claimed the God of the Jewish Bible was different from the God of Christian experience. Church authorities declared Marcion to be a heretic. Church authorities have not always been right in their judgments, but they were on this one!

We still hear contemporary Christians claim that the Old Testament evidences a God of wrath and the New Testament a God of love. Those persons who make such declarations have not read either testament closely enough. Christians have used this misinterpretation over centuries to oppress and even to murder Jews.

The reasons Christian should read the Old Testament are many, including the following:

- Jesus was a Jew. His scriptures were largely what Christians now call the Old Testament.
- The New Testament is filled with references to the Old. The Christian Bible is unintelligible without the Hebrew Bible (another name for the Old Testament).
- The Bible, Old and New Testaments, contains dialogues, conversations, and arguments that later writers carried on with former writers. Christians should read the whole scriptures in order to enter the conversations and debates responsibly.
- The Bible has been an important influence in U.S. public life, but the more influential testament has been the Old!
- Christianity has a violent history against Judaism. Contemporary Christians should seek to avoid all vestiges of anti-Judaism, including the claim of having eclipsed Judaism (against which, for example, Paul certainly claimed the opposite; see Romans 9—11).

## Jarrod McKenna

### Who is...
**Jarrod McKenna**

*I hate Scrabble (I'm dyslexic).*

One way to resist the co-opting of Christ into a consumer self-help trinket by those pedaling false salvations that seek to sedate us so we sleep soundly through the destruction of God's good creation (almost as if the resurrection never happened) is to be immersed in the Hebrew Bible until its stories become our own. This is not an easy thing to do.

There are many modern-day Marcionite heresies, both fundamentalist and liberal, that seek to kidnap Christ from his prophetic Jewishness, divorcing his life from the Hebraic hope of the redemption of not just souls, but all of creation. The New Testament is too easily co-opted when it is cut off from its context as the nonviolent fulfillment of the hopes of Israel, in Jesus.

This ripping of the roots of the New Testament from the fertile soil of the Old Testament leaves us with emaciated imaginations, susceptible to predatory forces seeking to feed us death-dealing spiritualities of otherworldly escapism.

Like the early church, we must become communities that immerse people foreign to the Old Testament into the Hebraic hope that has been fulfilled in a Messiah who saves with a towel of service, not a sword of war—who defeats his enemies by suffering for them rather than making them suffer.

As the Mishnah (Mishnah Pesachim 10:5) instructs, "In every generation, [people] must so regard themselves as if they themselves came out of Egypt, for it is written, 'And thou shalt tell thy children on that day saying, it is because of that which the LORD did for me when I came forth out of Egypt' (Ex. 13:8)." We must ourselves follow the resurrected Christ out of captivity into the kingdom that is breaking into history, bringing heaven to earth.

## Jim L. Robinson

The question may be related to another issue, namely, the distinction between law and grace. Virtually all New Testament teaching acknowledges such a distinction, and speaks of the law as the "old covenant" and grace as the "new covenant."

But the contrast between the "old and new covenants" is not the same as a comparison between the Hebrew and Christian scriptures (which we typically call the Old Testament and New Testament).

While it's true that the Hebrew scriptures (the Old Testament) are an account of a people living under the covenant of law, and the Christian scriptures (the New Testament) give witness to the covenant of grace, the distinctions are not directly related in a one-to-one correlation.

To read the New Testament divorced from its connection to the Old is like coming into a movie at the halfway point. The "story" is not complete if you leave out any of it. While the Bible is a collection of writings that span two millennia of oral and written traditions, there is a consistency that's almost miraculous; moreover, a central theme of the New Testament is that Jesus is the "fulfillment" of the Old.

Apart from the context of the Old Testament—especially in a consumer culture obsessed with individualism—the meaning of Jesus' crucifixion is reduced to the status of personal opinion. And while everyone is entitled to an opinion, that doesn't necessarily serve truth.

## Marcia Ford

The Old Testament is much more than a record of events that happened before the time of Christ. It contains a great deal of information about Jewish history, customs, and rituals that help us make sense of much of the New Testament.

By understanding Jewish culture, we can better understand why some people readily accepted—or rejected—Christ. And of special significance to Christians are the many Old Testament prophecies that were fulfilled in the person of Jesus.

Most important, perhaps, is that the Old Testament is considered to be the word of God just as is the New Testament. Jewish rabbis and scholars deemed the books of what we call the Old Testament worthy to become their scriptures, something we shouldn't take lightly.

Jesus obviously recognized the value of those scriptures, quoting them and referring to them throughout his ministry. The work of those Jewish leaders gave the early church fathers a solid foundation for discerning the canon of the New Testament.

Finally, to dismiss the Old Testament as irrelevant to Christians would mean eliminating from our common spiritual heritage such content as the Psalms; the always stirring stories of Abraham, Joseph, Esther, and others; the book of Proverbs, and so much more—including the Ten Commandments, which throughout history has served as a set of guiding principles for much of humanity.

## Scriptural References

Matthew 1:22; 2:5, 15, 17, 23; Psalm 19:7–9, 22; Isaiah 55:10–11; Romans 9—11; 2 Timothy 3:14–17; 1 Peter 1:22–25; Revelation 22:18–19

## Suggested Additional Sources for Reading

- Rob Bell and Don Golden, *Jesus Wants to Save Christians: A Manifesto for the Church in Exile* (Zondervan, 2008).
- Mary C. Boys and Sara S. Lee, *Christians and Jews in Dialogue: Learning in the Presence of the Other* (Skylight Paths Publishing, 2008).
- Steve Bridge, *Getting the Old Testament: What It Meant to Them, What It Means for Us* (Hendrickson, 2009).
- Walter Brueggemann, *The Prophetic Imagination,* 2d edition (Fortress Press, 2001).
- Ellen F. Davis and Richard B. Hays, eds., *The Art of Reading Scripture* (Eerdmans, 2003).
- Mark Driscoll, *On the Old Testament (A Book You'll Actually Read)* (Crossway, 2008).
- John Goldingay, *Old Testament Theology: Israel's Gospel* (InterVarsity Press, 2003).
- Darrell Jodock, ed., *Covenantal Conversations: Christians in Dialogue with Jews and Judaism* (Fortress Press, 2008).
- Melody D. Knowles, ed., *Contesting Texts: Jews and Christians in Conversation about the Bible* (Fortress Press, 2007).
- Stephen J. Lennox, *God's Story Revealed: A Guide for Understanding the Old Testament* (Wesleyan Publishing House, 2009).
- Christopher J. H. Wright, *Walking in the Ways of the Lord* (InterVarsity Press, 1996).

## Suggested Questions for Further Discussion/Thought

1. What is your impression of the Old Testament? How was this impression formed?
2. What can happen when Christians pick up parts of the Old Testament without reading or understanding it? Give some examples.
3. Is the God of the Old Testament different from the God of the New Testament? Why or why not?
4. What part of the Old Testament is the biggest turnoff for you?
5. How has the Old Testament enriched your spiritual life? Helped you understand the New Testament? Confirmed to you that Jesus is who he says he is?

*Does the Bible ever refer to itself as "the Bible"? If not, where did the name "Bible" come from?*

## Jason Boyett

Biblical writers refer many times to "the scriptures" or "the Law and the Prophets" or "the Word of God." But you won't find any references to "the Bible" in the Old or New Testaments. That's because "Bible" isn't a biblical word.

To begin with, it's English, and the Bible was written primarily in Hebrew and Greek. Around the third century, people began referring to the Christian scriptures as *ta biblia ta hagia* (the holy books), a phrase that comes from *byblion*, the Greek word describing the Egyptian papyrus plant that was used back then to make paper. The word *byblion* derived from an ancient city, Byblos, the Phoenician port through which most of the Egyptian papyrus was exported. (Byblos became modern-day Gebal, Lebanon.)

Anyway, without getting too deeply into etymology, the Greek phrasing evolved into the Latin *biblia sacra* (holy books) and at some point in the Middle Ages the Latin became Anglicized into the English word Bible.

## Jim L. Robinson

No. The word, "Bible" derives from a Greek word that means "book." Some texts refer to the scriptures, but never "in the first person." The New Testament references to scripture proceed primarily from the first five books of the Old Testament (called the Pentateuch), some of the writings of the Prophets, and some of the wisdom writings of the Old Testament.

## Marcia Ford

The Bible never refers to itself using that term because the term didn't come into use until several centuries after the last book of the Bible had been written. The word "Bible"—which is always capitalized when referring to the Word of God—stems from a Greek word meaning "book." Once the early church fathers determined which books written by or attributed to followers of God were authentic and worthy to be considered the Word of God, that collection of sixty-six books became known as the book—the Bible.

While the Bible had been considered a sacred or holy book from its very inception, the specific term "Holy Bible" first appeared on what we call the

King James Bible—known more accurately as the Authorized Version, so named because in 1604 King James I of England authorized the new translation. It was completed in 1611.

Although the Bible does not call itself by that name, several verses do mention other portions of the Bible. In one particular passage, Jesus refers to the first five books of the Bible (the Law) and the scriptural writings of the prophets: "Do not think that I have come to abolish the Law or the Prophets; I have not come to abolish them but to fulfill them. I tell you the truth, until heaven and earth disappear, not the smallest letter, not the least stroke of a pen, will by any means disappear from the Law until everything is accomplished" (Mt. 5:17–18, NIV).

## Scriptural References

Isaiah 40:8; 2 Timothy 3:15–16; Romans 16:26; 2 Peter 1:20–21, 3:15–16; Daniel 9:2; Matthew 4:3–4, 6; 21:13; 22:29; 26:24; Luke 24:44; Acts 13:15; Ephesians 5:26; Hebrews 4:12; 1 Thessalonians 2:13

## Suggested Additional Sources for Reading

- AllAboutTruth: http://www.AllAboutTruth.org (articles and videos about the Bible).
- Biblical Studies Foundation: http://www.Bible.org.
- Online Etymology Dictionary: http://www.etymonline.com/index. php?term=bible.

## Suggested Questions for Further Discussion/Thought

1. Do you think the biblical writers knew, as they wrote their prophecies, letters, and historical accounts, that they were writing what would one day be considered scripture?
2. Do you view the Bible more as one complete book or as a collection?
3. Is there a translation of the Bible that you consider more or less legitimate or authoritative? Why?

# uestion

*How do we reconcile the Old Testament command for vengeance (eye for an eye) with Jesus' command to turn the other cheek and love our enemies?*

## Becky Garrison

### Who is...
**Becky Garrison**

*I'm an urban flyfisher and kayaker.*

Our hatred of the "other" is nothing new. At the time of Jesus' birth, the Samaritans and the Jews had been at each other's throats for literally hundreds of years. At the time when Jesus told the parable of the Good Samaritan (Lk. 10:25–37), the concept of a Samaritan coming to the rescue of a Jew would have been considered just as incongruous as if, say, a Focus on the Family follower marched in the New York City LGBT (Lesbian, Gay, Bisexual, and Transgender) Pride Parade today.

But as the parable made clear, the Samaritan was considered the Jewish man's "neighbor." By implication, that means the definition of "neighbor" has to be expanded to include all of God's children, including those of different social classes, races, creeds, and political affiliations. When Jesus commanded his followers to "go and do likewise" by following the example of the Good Samaritan, he challenged the early church to look beyond its comfort zone. His disciples were required to obey the greatest commandment by showing Jesus' love and kindness to all people because everyone was their "neighbor."

The early Christian church cut across the various hierarchical lines that divided people. It did not seek to dominate the political establishment or maintain the status quo; rather, its goal was to spread the universal love of Christ. In doing that, it transformed the world.

## Jarrod McKenna

I had just finished running a workshop for Greenpeace, The Wilderness Society, and an antinuclear organization on the history and power of nonviolent direct action in which I had explored and trained people in the transformative nonviolence of Gandhi, Martin Luther

King Jr., and to the surprise of many gathered, Jesus. Afterwards a well-respected activist approached me away from others and asked tearfully, "Why was this Jesus not found in my experience of church?"

This question goes to the heart of the gospel, to the heart of mission, and to the heart of discipleship. Why is it that people can't find the hope of the world in our churches? I think it's directly connected to the lack of schooling in letting God's love through us by "loving our enemies"—to be merciful as the triune God is merciful. Fierce Calvary-shaped love is how God has saved us and it's how we are to witness to our salvation. Grace is both how God has saved us and the pattern of kingdom living for which the Holy Spirit empowers us.

"Eye for an eye" is not about vengeance but the limitation of retaliation. In Christ, violence is not only restrained but also transformed. On the cross, God does not overcome evil with evil but with good (Rom. 12:21). There is nothing passive about Jesus' turning the other cheek in the face of injustice (Jn. 18:23). To turn the other cheek is to practice the provocative peace that embodies the healing justice of the kingdom by exposing injustice with the presence of love (Col. 2:15).

We don't need to reconcile vengeance or violence with loving our enemies. Instead, we need to be open to the Holy Spirit's empowerment to witness to God's reconciling the world to Godself through the nonviolent Messiah, Jesus.

## Rebecca Bowman Woods

In *Religious Literacy: What Every American Needs to Know and Doesn't*, Stephen Prothero shares the story of a 1995 Colorado murder trial. During deliberations, one juror pulled out his Bible and quoted Leviticus 24, the "eye for an eye" passage that concludes with "He that killeth a man, he shall be put to death." After the juror instructed his fellow jurors to go home and prayerfully consider this passage, they voted unanimously for the death penalty.

The state Supreme Court ordered a new trial, ruling that jurors were not allowed to consult the Bible. Some Christians, led by Colorado-based Focus on the Family, protested the higher court's ruling—perhaps rightly so. Can a court really prevent people of faith from including scripture in their decision making?

But the real injustice, in Prothero's opinion, was that the jurors failed to consider the rest of the Bible, particularly Jesus' views on retaliation in Matthew 5:38–42.

"There are very few passages from the Hebrew Bible that are explicitly refuted in the New Testament, but Leviticus 24:20–21 (echoed in Ex. 21:23–25 and Deut. 19:21) is one of them," writes Prothero, a professor of religious studies at Boston University and a staunch advocate of religious literacy.

Christians should rarely fall back on the argument that the "New Testament supersedes the Old Testament." In Matthew 5, Jesus warns that he has not "come to abolish the law or the prophets" but to fulfill them. He teaches an ethic that "embraces and extends" the law in several instances and refutes it in a few.

Amy Greenbaum, a friend who is in the process of becoming an ordained Reformed rabbi, says the "eye for an eye" text in Leviticus 24 would not have been taken literally, even in ancient times.

## Kathy Escobar

### Who is...
#### Kathy Escobar

*To me, people slurping or swallowing loudly is like nails on a chalkboard. Worst pet peeve.*

I started seeking God on my own when I was a little girl, apart from my family who were not Christians. I can't explain it, really; I was always drawn to Jesus but couldn't quite make sense of the Old Testament and a lot of the crazy things that were in there—whole communities being wiped out, God's vengeance being poured out left and right. I tried to skip over those parts and somehow erase them from my mind and just focus on Jesus because that was a lot more comforting.

Later, as I began to mature in my faith, I realized I needed to wrestle with this disparity. I admit that I still do. I rest on the new order that Jesus created through the incarnation, turning the old ways upside down. I think the contrast is important; the radical difference between vengeance in the Old and New Testaments makes God's point. Jesus changes everything, teaching what the Kingdom now means.

The Sermon on the Mount clearly sets the stage for this new way that completely demolishes the idea of "an eye for an eye." I don't think I have to pick apart all the reasons why the Old Testament contains certain stories or examples that are utterly confusing and seemingly contrary to God's heart for people. I try to rest on the reality that through the gospels, all that changed. The commands shifted, the law got summed up, and the kingdom principles that Jesus taught were going to be much harder to apply than the old laws by a long shot.

## Scriptural References

Exodus 21:12–26; Leviticus 24:10–23; Matthew 5:3–10, 17–48; 22:37–40, 51;
Mark 12:28–31; Luke 6; Romans 5:10, 11; 12

## Suggested Additional Sources for Reading

- Dave Andrews, *Plan Be* (published by the author).
- Gregory Boyd, *The Myth of the Christian Religion: Losing your Religion for the Beauty of a Revolution* (Zondervan, 2009).
- Lee C. Camp, *Mere Discipleship: Radical Christianity in a Rebellious World* (Brazos, 2008).
- Becky Garrison, *Red and Blue God, Black and Blue Church* (Jossey-Bass, 2006).
- Kirk Johnson, "Colorado Court Bars Execution Because Jurors Consulted Bible," *The New York Times*, March 29, 2005: http://www.nytimes.com/2005/03/29/national/29bible.html.
- Martin Luther King Jr., *Strength to Love* (Fortress Press, 2010).
- Stephen Prothero, *Religious Literacy: What Every American Needs to Know and Doesn't* (HarperOne, 2008).
- Stephen Prothero's Web site: http://www.stephenprothero.com.
- Desmond Tutu, *No Future without Forgiveness* (Image, 2000).
- Miroslav Volf, *Exclusion and Embrace* (Abingdon Press, 1996).
- N. T. Wright, *Evil and the Justice of God* (InterVarsity Press, 2009).

## Suggested Questions for Further Discussion/Thought

1. What are some of the problems with living out Jesus' "turn the other cheek" ethic?
2. Is killing another human being acceptable for Christians under certain circumstances, or should Christians oppose the death penalty?
3. How is Jesus' summation of the law—"Loving God, loving others as ourselves"—harder than the Old Testament laws?
4. What does it mean that we are called to love as God has loved us?
5. Have you had people ask you why a Jesus who dies for his enemies isn't taught in church?

# Question

*Is there a right or wrong way to read the Bible?*

## Jason Boyett

### Who is...
**Jason Boyett**

*I am a triathlete.*

A. The easiest way to answer that question is to go negative: how not to read the Bible. If you've never read much of the Bible before, don't start on page 1 and try to slog your way through it. The Bible isn't a novel. The beginning, Genesis, is fascinating but you'll lose traction in Leviticus and be completely stuck by the time you get to Numbers.

Don't read the Bible as if it is life's instruction manual. Though it's full of wisdom in books like Proverbs or passages like the Sermon on the Mount, the Bible is not an advice book. Nor is it merely a devotional guide from a single author or a history book about a particular time and place. No, the Bible is a mishmash of literary genres, written across centuries of time by dozens of authors, each with a distinct audience and purpose.

What's the right way to read the Bible? Read it as the revelation of God and God's relationship with his people. It's a messy relationship, colored with sin, failure, sacrifice, salvation, redemption, love, and surprising grace. The Bible has much to say about its own context as well as about our world today, but don't diminish it by thinking of it as a novel, a history book, or an instruction manual. It is those things in part, but on the whole, it is so much more: the great story of God.

## Jim L. Robinson

### Who is...
#### Jim L. Robinson

*After high school, I was a barber for several years.
Some interesting heads I've trimmed include "Dandy"
Don Meredith and Tom Landry of the Dallas
Cowboys, and General Creighton Abrams, Head of
Military Assistance Command in Vietnam.*

Absolutely. There is a strong tendency to read the scriptures, not in order to hear what the scriptures say (which is the "right" way to read them), but rather to verify what is already believed about the scriptures (which is the wrong way to read them.) The former is called exegesis and latter is called eisegesis.

## Joshua Einsohn

Perhaps it's naïve to think that everyone would start reading the Bible with a critical eye, but I believe that all people should read the Bible and try to decide its meaning, as much as they are able, for themselves. Ideally, religious leaders should be there to help facilitate an individual's reading of the Bible, not predigest their flock's faith for them. They should help guide, not impose.

Many people seem to fear what they might discover if they ask too many questions, but the most comfortably faithful folks that I've met have spent a great deal of time rigorously questioning their main religious texts alone or with their friends and their community. The more they struggle with the stories and discover their meanings, the more they find themselves comfortable and secure in their faith.

One of the most interesting Jewish ceremonies I've attended included a "questions from the audience" segment for members of the congregation who had questions about a passage and needed some group debate to help them sort out their thoughts. The people who asked the questions and engaged in debate had clearly spent time thinking on their own before they came in. Their religious leaders and other members in the community helped them to clarify their thinking.

It isn't diminishing one's faith to ask questions about the Bible in order to reach a deeper, more comfortable understanding.

## José F. Morales Jr.

There are right and wrong ways to read the Bible. I used to move within certain church circles that said there was objective Truth (with a capital "T"). Because of "objective Truth," they argued that logically there could only be one way to read scripture.

I later discovered that the only way was their way, and that their way was laden with a racist and classist agenda: protecting the status quo of the white suburban dominance. Although John 8:32 says the truth will set you free, as a Latino from "da 'hood," there was nothing freeing to me about their readings.

At the other end of the spectrum, postmodernism challenges this idea of objective Truth, and claims at its most extreme that there is no truth. Theologian Catherine Keller, in *On the Mystery* (Fortress Press, 2008), has labeled these two extremes "absolute" and "dissolute." She argues that neither is helpful nor faithful.

I always refer to the story in Luke 10 of the lawyer who asks Jesus, "What must I do to inherit eternal life?" Jesus then answers with a question, "What is written in the law? What do you read there?" The Good News Bible paraphrases the second question: "How do you interpret it?" In other words, what's the right way to read the scriptures? The lawyer answers correctly, "Love God . . . love neighbor." St. Augustine, that great early church father, put it succinctly when he said that any reading of the Bible that gets in the way of loving God and/or neighbor is a wrong interpretation.

We read the Bible to be freed to love, to be empowered to love. To understand what this "love" thing really is, I recommend starting with the Bible.

## Joshua Toulouse

While there no doubt are traditions that will tell you exactly how the Bible is to be read, the Bible doesn't come with a how-to manual. All anyone can really give you on this question is her or his own opinion, so the easy answer is no, there is no explicitly right or wrong way to read the Bible.

Some people read the Bible to find answers on what exactly they should believe about moral issues, some for inspiration, and others to learn more about where their religion came from or as a guide for where it should be headed. All of these are legitimate ways of reading the Bible, and we all can find ourselves responding to the Bible in any or all of these ways, as well as others, at different points in our lives, and that is completely acceptable.

To get the most out of the Bible, use the many commentaries available to learn more about the historical context that shaped the writing of the books. It is also helpful to recognize that there are different understandings of how various words and phrases should be translated, and that these different translations can dramatically change what meaning we get from the text.

While very few of us have time to learn Hebrew and Greek—the languages in which the Bible was originally written—luckily, there are people who do have time, and we can avail ourselves of their hard work and discover for ourselves which of the many theories we agree with and which theories fit the best with our own theology.

## Scriptural References

Psalm 119:14–16; Luke 24:32; 10:25–37; 1 Corinthians 13:1–2; 2 Timothy 3:16

## Suggested Additional Sources for Reading

- Marcus J. Borg, *Reading the Bible again for the First Time: Taking the Bible Seriously but Not Literally* (Harper San Francisco, 2002).
- John A. Buehrens, *Understanding the Bible: An Introduction for Skeptics, Seekers, and Religious Liberals* (Beacon, 2004).
- Bart D. Ehrman, *Jesus, Interrupted: Revealing the Hidden Contradictions in the Bible (and Why We Don't Know about Them)* (HarperOne, 2010).
- Peter J. Gomes, *The Good Book: Reading the Bible with Mind and Heart* (HarperOne, 2002).
- Justo L. González, *Santa Biblia: The Bible through Hispanic Eyes* (Abingdon Press, 1996).
- Alister McGrath, *In the Beginning: The Story of the King James Bible and How It Changed a Nation, a Language, and a Culture* (Anchor, 2002).
- David Plotz, *Good Book: The Bizarre, Hilarious, Disturbing, Marvelous, and Inspiring Things I Learned When I Read Every Single Word of the Bible* (Harper Perennial, 2010).
- *Ryken's Bible Handbook: A Guide to Reading and Studying the Bible* (Tyndale, 2005).
- R. S. Sugirtharajah, ed., *Voices from the Margins: Interpreting the Bible in the Third World* (Orbis Books, 2006).
- N. T. Wright, *The Last Word: Scripture and the Authority of God—Getting beyond the Bible Wars* (HarperOne, 2006).

## Suggested Questions for Further Discussion/Thought

1. What kind of risks would be involved if you set aside all preconceived ideas about scripture and approached it as if for the first time?
2. What is "truth"? And how do you know it is truth?
3. Is it wrong to read the Bible with a critical eye? Don't faith leaders do that?
4. Is it possible to come to a different conclusion than your religion does about certain passages without losing your faith or violating the rules of your religion?
5. How should the original context of the various biblical texts shape what they mean to contemporary society?

*How do we reconcile the two different "creation stories" presented in Genesis chapters one and two?*

## José F. Morales Jr.

If one thinks that Genesis 1—2 literally happened (i.e., is historical fact), then the two cannot be reconciled for they are starkly different:

- In Genesis 1, it takes seven days. In Genesis 2, we're not given a timeframe but it feels like everything up to the forming of Adam happened in one day.
- The order in which things are made (plants, humans, animals, etc.) is different in each account.
- The writing styles are different in each, including syntax, word choice, and verb tenses.
- The name for God is different in each: "Elohim" in the first and "Yahweh Elohim" in the second.
- In Genesis 1, God is transcendent, in the "beyond" somewhere. There's only a voice. In Genesis 2, God is very "human," walking in the garden, getting dirt under her or his nails, and so on.

These stories were not intended to be a science textbook. They are myths. Don't be shocked! I don't mean "myth" the way we commonly use it—"Oh, that's just a myth!"—but the way that anthropologists use it. A "myth" is a story that makes sense of reality at its deepest level.

The creation myths serve to give theological meaning to existence, not to give scientific explanations. To quote Marcus Borg's *The Heart of Christianity*, the creation stories are not literally true, but they are really true. Genesis 1 speaks of God's mystery and grandeur, of the universe's mystery and goodness, and of humanity's divine essence. Genesis 2 reveals God's intimacy and closeness and the interconnectedness of all things, including how humanity (adam) and the earth (adamah) with which we're formed share a bond. That's why I don't tell people to "go green" but instead to rediscover our inherent greenness.

Let science tell us "how." Let the creation myths tell us "why."

## Craig Detweiler

**Who is...**
**Craig Detweiler**

*I collect baseball cards.*

The Bible is loaded with multiple accounts of the same events. The books of Kings and Chronicles offer two different ways of remembering events in the history of Israel. One celebrates the glory of kings while the other takes a more skeptical approach to sovereigns. The gospels of Matthew, Mark, and Luke recount similar stories in the life of Jesus, adding in unique emphases and details. The authors appealed to particular audiences. The creation stories in Genesis give us two ways of understanding who we are and where we've come from.

The first chapter of Genesis offers a cosmic take on creation, from chaotic waters to the forming of land and animals. God's activity unfolds across seven distinct days. Humanity arises on the sixth day as the dramatic crown of God's creation. It also concludes with Sabbath rest. The shape of our work-week stems from this seminal passage.

The second chapter of Genesis (actually starting with Gen. 2:4) cuts almost directly to Adam and Eve. It fills in more details about their relationship with each other and their creator. It defines the boundaries of the Garden of Eden and describes Adam and Eve's role as caretakers. It also includes the fall of humanity, where they put themselves at the center of the garden, unseating the primacy of God in their lives. We get the birth of shame and blame. The heights of Genesis 1 collapse in the depths of Genesis 3. A glorious setup unravels in an inability to respect certain space set up as off limits.

The first creation story gives us nature's glory and God's rhythms. The second creation story gives us the beauty of relationships and the ache that arises when trust is broken.

## Joshua Toulouse

Most modern biblical scholars agree that Genesis was written by various authors and later edited into one book. The two creation stories with their conflicting order of events and wildly different styles support this. What we as modern readers can do with these two divergent stories is to recognize that neither is meant to be a historical account of the creation of the world, but rather important stories about the relationship of our God with the world and with humanity.

Both of these stories cast our God as Creator, an important designation. Both are centered on the creation of humanity and our importance in the world. In the first, God gives us dominion over the world and everything in it (Gen. 1:28–30), an incredible responsibility that should speak to us now as much as, if not more than, it did to those who first told and heard this story. It also helps to set up the idea of the Sabbath, an important part of the Jewish faith.

In the second, the creation of humanity comes before the creation of anything else. Also, out of the second story comes the genealogy that will lead to Abraham and even later, to Jesus, setting up the personal relationship that we have with God.

We are given a story that shows us creation on a large scale and that highlights the power and goodness of our creator, and we are given a story that centers on humanity, the beginning of our relationship with that creator. Both have important places in our beliefs.

## Christian Piatt

### Who is...
### Christian Piatt

*In college, I was the lead singer for several rock bands and had hair down to my waist.*

In Genesis 1, man and woman are created at the same time. In Genesis 2, however, God creates Eve from the rib of Adam. Although both stories address the questions of how we got here, the first is a broader, more "cosmic" approach to the issue of creation. And while the Adam and Eve story is in many ways more accessible for readers, it also has some pretty clear agendas.

First, the Adam and Eve story tries to explain the nature of sin, describing metaphorically how humanity has screwed up since day one and how God allows us the ability to make choices on our own, good or bad. But the story also places the man in a superior role over women, which makes sense given the patriarchal culture in which this story would have originated.

Finally, the story deftly combines these first two items basically to blame women for leading guys astray. Though both sexes pay a price for their shortcomings, it's the women who have to endure the pains of childbirth as penance for tempting males in their fall from grace.

One has to wonder how differently the story might read if written by women. Maybe our penance would be lifting heavy things for all eternity and suffering the consequences of never asking directions.

# Becky Garrison

A. According to Francis Collins, Director of the National Institute of Health, "Despite twenty-five centuries of debate, it is fair to say that no human knows what the meaning of Genesis 1 and 2 was precisely intended to be." At the risk of doing a major disservice to centuries of biblical criticism, one can say that obtaining empirical evidence from a book including, but not limited to, narrative, poetry, epistle, apocalyptic literature, and legal texts clearly misses the meaning behind these messages.

Simon Conway Morris, professor of earth sciences at Cambridge University, is right when he proclaims, "I think if you try and make the Bible into a quasi-scientific document, you're doing it great disservice, if not violence. And you're also distorting, if not maligning, science, which is an attempt to understand the world as we see it."

New Testament scholar and Anglican bishop N. T. Wright adds this theological tidbit: "The Bible isn't there simply to be an accurate reference point for people who want to look things up and be sure they got them right. It is there to equip people to carry forth [God's] purposes of new covenant and new creation."

## Scriptural References

Genesis 1—2; Job 38, 39; Psalm 19:1–6

## Suggested Additional Sources for Reading

- Francisco J. Ayala, *Darwin and Intelligent Design* (Fortress Press, 2006).
- Marcus J. Borg, *Reading the Bible again for the First Time: Taking the Bible Seriously but Not Literally* (Harper San Francisco, 2002), especially chap. 4, "Reading the Creation Stories Again."
- Francis S. Collins, *The Language of God: A Scientist Presents Evidence for Belief* (Free Press, 2007).
- Becky Garrison's selection was adapted from her book *The New Atheist Crusaders and Their Unholy Grail: The Misguided Quest to Destroy Your Faith* (Thomas Nelson, 2008).
- Stephen W. Hawking, *The Theory of Everything: The Origin and Fate of the Universe* (Jaico Publishing House, 2007).
- Kenneth R. Miller, *Finding Darwin's God* (Harper Perennial, 2007).

- *New Interpreter's Study Bible: Genesis* (Abingdon Press, 2003).
- Joan Roughgarden, *Evolution and Christian Faith: Reflections of an Evolutionary Biologist* (Island Press, 2006).
- Barbara Brown Taylor, *The Luminous Web: Essays on Science and Religion* (Cowley, 2000).

## Suggested Questions for Further Discussion/Thought

1. Does the theory of evolution challenge or confirm your faith in a Creator God? How so?
2. In Genesis 1, God is transcendent, in the "beyond"—God is *big*. In Genesis 2, God is very close, with human-like qualities. Which of these two images resonates more with your view of God? Why?
3. From the character Stan Marsh on *South Park*: "Couldn't evolution be the answer to how and not the answer to why?"

*Since the Bible isn't in alphabetical or chronological order, how did it get in its current order?*

## Marcia Ford

That depends on which Bible you're referring to. The Roman Catholic canon of scripture includes some books that Protestant Bibles exclude, and in Eastern Orthodox Bibles, some books appear in a different order.

Generally, though, the books of the Bible are arranged according to the Jewish tradition of keeping various types of books together and arranging them chronologically within that type. Genesis through Deuteronomy contains the basic precepts God gave to the Israelites, which are known as the Law. Joshua through Esther outlines the subsequent history of the nation of Israel. Job through Song of Solomon incorporates poetry and wisdom literature. The writings of the "major" prophets—those whose messages were of critical importance—are found in Isaiah through Daniel; the "minor" prophets' writings, Hosea through Malachi, come last in the Old Testament.

The New Testament follows suit; its books are also arranged by type. The history books, Matthew through Acts, tell the stories of Jesus and the founding of the church. Romans through Jude includes letters written by early church leaders to churches in other areas and to individuals. Revelation is the New Testament's book of prophecy.

The order just described generally applies to Bibles used for worship, in group settings, and the like. For private study, however, you can find study Bibles in which the books are arranged chronologically, which helps you navigate your way through the world of the Bible and discover what else was going on when major events occurred.

## Joshua Toulouse

The order of the Old Testament in the Christian Bible is slightly different from the order of the Jewish Bible, although the books included are the same. As Warren Carter, my New Testament professor in seminary, liked to point out, there was no one keeping minutes while the canonical discussions were taking place in the first four hundred years of the Christian movement.

The books in the Bible are placed together by genre. In some of those genres, there are attempts at chronological ordering. Of course, the actual chronology of when the books were written isn't always perfectly clear, either. Some believe that the order of the gospels in the Bible is the order in which they were written, but most theologians agree that Mark was actually the first gospel written, not Matthew.

As for the letters in the New Testament, they were ordered with the community letters first, from longest to shortest, then the personal letters, longest to shortest. There was some push for the letters to be ordered chronologically, but just as with the gospels, the chronological order believed then and the chronological order argued for now is not always the same. The dates of many of the letters are hotly contested.

# José F. Morales Jr.

The biblical scholar Brevard Childs said that the order of scripture speaks to the purpose or function of each book or each section.

The gospels of Matthew and Luke copied large chunks from Mark, which came first, when writing their versions. So why is Matthew first in the New Testament? Since the beginning, the ancients referred to it as "the church's gospel." When you read it, you can see why. Matthew is concerned with church authority, instruction, and stability, ending with the Great Commission. Matthew is placed first in the New Testament to remind us that scripture is the church's book, and that the livelihood of the church depends on God's action in Christ.

Also, the way that Jews order the Old Testament, which they call the Tanakh, is telling. Protestants and Jews canonized the same books but put them in different order. For example, five books that are scattered throughout the Christian Bible are put together into one section in the Tanakh, called the "Five Scrolls." This was done because of the purpose they serve: They're read during the five major festivals of the Jewish faith:

- Song of Songs: Passover
- Ruth: Feast of Weeks (Pentecost)
- Lamentations: Ninth of Av (commemorates the destruction of the temple)
- Ecclesiastes: Feast of Booths
- Esther: Purim

Also, Protestants and Jews end the Old Testament/Tanakh differently. The Tanakh ends with Second Chronicles, which concludes with a promise of rebuilding the Temple in Jerusalem, central to most Jewish eschatology. Protestants end it with Malachi, which prophesizes the coming of the prophet

"Elijah" to "prepare the way for God," thus setting the stage for John the Baptizer and Jesus.

To quote the famous Chicago architect Louis Sullivan, "form follows function."

## Scriptural References

John 20:31; Romans 15:4; 2 Timothy 3:14–17

## Suggested Additional Sources for Reading

- Walter Brueggemann, *An Introduction to the Old Testament: The Canon and Christian Imagination* (Westminster John Knox Press, 2003), especially "Introduction: Imaginative Remembering."
- Walter Brueggemann, *Reverberations of Faith: A Theological Handbook of Old Testament Themes* (Westminster John Knox Press, 2002), especially "Festivals" and "Torah."
- Brevard S. Childs, *Biblical Theology: A Proposal* (Fortress Press, 2002).
- Craig A. Evans and Emanuel Tov, eds., *Exploring the Origins of the Bible* (Baker Academic, 2008).
- Luke Timothy Johnson, *The Writings of the New Testament: An Interpretation* (Fortress Press, 2002).
- *The Life and Times Historical Reference Bible* (Thomas Nelson, 1997).
- Lee Martin McDonald, *The Biblical Canon: Its Origin, Transmission, and Authority* (Hendrickson, 2007).

## Suggested Questions for Further Discussion/Thought

1. How would you like to see the books of the Bible arranged—alphabetically, chronologically, or possibly some other way? Which way do you think would be most helpful to you in your study of the Bible?
2. Why do you think that early Jewish scholars arranged the books of the Hebrew scriptures (our Old Testament) by literary type? The early church leaders followed their lead. Why do you think they chose to do so?
3. Read John 20:31, Romans 15:4, and 2 Timothy 3:14–17. According to these passages, what is the purpose and function of scripture? Do you agree or disagree? Why?

# Is there a scriptural basis for God changing God's mind? Why?

## David J. Lose

**Who is...**
**David J. Lose**

*I'm a sixth-generation Lutheran pastor.*

Yes. At several places in scripture, God enters into dialogue with humans—Abraham and Moses, for instance—and seems to change God's mind.

At first blush, this can be a little unsettling. I mean, isn't God supposed to be absolutely consistent, unchanging, and unmovable? Isn't part of what we look for in God a kind of rock-solid permanence? Finally—and here, I think, is the ultimate question—can we trust a God who changes God's own mind?

Before answering this question, it's crucial to remember that God typically changes God's mind in and through conversation with God's people. That's important because it means that the relationship we have with God is a real relationship. Lots of Christians talk about having a relationship with God, but for a relationship to be genuine there needs to be (1) ongoing conversation and (2) the possibility for growth and change on both sides. The biblical witness portrays a God who enters into a real relationship and cares enough about us to change.

So can we trust a God who changes God's mind? Well, we can trust that God will hang in there with us, keeping the conversation going even when it gets difficult. We can trust that God won't give up on us. We can trust that God will take us seriously and even be affected by us. We can trust that God wants a real relationship with us and will go to great lengths to be in relationship with us. In many ways, that's what the cross is all about: God loving us enough to suffer and die for us. And when it comes to loving us, that's one thing scripture promises God will never change God's mind about.

Yes, I think we can trust this kind of God.

## Rebecca Bowman Woods

**Who is...**
### Rebecca Bowman Woods

*I have watched the soap opera* All My Children *off and on since it began.*

The book of Jonah contains one of the best-known examples of God changing God's mind. This Sunday school staple about a prophet's reluctance to go and warn the people of Nineveh that they are about to be destroyed is probably not historically accurate, but that's beside the point. Although Jonah is often read as a gentle warning not to try to escape God's calling (unless you like being thrown overboard and swallowed by a fish), it also contrasts human compassion (with its limitations, expectations, and baggage) with God's compassion.

God seemed intent on destroying Nineveh and the people who lived there, but they repented—from the king on down to the farm animals (hint: Animals in sackcloth and ashes might be a humorous touch on the author's part). So "God changed his mind about the calamity that he had said he would bring upon them; and he did not do it." (Jon. 3:10b).

One of my favorite examples of God changing God's mind (if your definition of God includes Jesus) is found in Mark 7:24–30. A Syrophoenician woman, a Gentile, approaches Jesus and asks him to rid her daughter of a demon. Jesus' response is shocking: "Let the children be fed first, for it is not fair to take the children's food and throw it to the dogs." In other words, his mission and ministry are primarily for his own people, not outsiders like her. She turns his answer around, reminding him that "even the dogs under the table eat the children's crumbs." Not only does Jesus change his mind; he tells her that it's because of what she said.

What is interesting to me is that in both cases, God (Jesus) changes God's mind to extend mercy and to be more inclusive. It would be interesting to see if this holds true for the rest of the Bible.

## Brandon Gilvin

### Who is...
**Brandon Gilvin**

*I have a thing for Pad Thai.*

In Genesis 18, the story of the destruction of Sodom and Gomorrah includes an interesting quip of a tradition. God reveals to Abraham that the cities have been judged as wicked and will be destroyed. Abraham essentially lobbies God to spare Sodom, arguing that if fifty righteous people can be found there, then the city should be spared. When God agrees, Abraham negotiates, whittling the number from fifty to twenty to ten. God agrees each time, amending the plan to destroy the city under any circumstance. Of course, Lot is the only righteous man, and only he and his household are spared.

There are other stories to this effect, and it's important to remember that the God portrayed in the Hebrew Bible is not the "Unmoved Mover" of Aristotle, nor is the God portrayed in most Western philosophy. This God functions like a character in relationship with human characters, involved intimately, and reacting to their actions as well as pressing them into action.

## José F. Morales Jr.

### Who is...
**José F. Morales Jr.**

*I think graffiti is legitimate art and should be treated as such.*

Here are two examples from scripture of God changing God's mind:

Exodus 32:14—"And the Lord changed his mind about the disaster that he planned to bring on his people." Here, God is angry at the idolatrous people and is about to "consume" them all. But Moses implores, and God heeds his plea.

Jonah 3:10—"When God saw what they did, how they turned from their evil ways, God changed his mind about the calamity that he had said he would bring upon them; and he did not do it." Sent by God, Jonah preaches God's doom on the Ninevites. But Nineveh repents. And God recants.

Traditional theology is troubled by this notion of God's mind-changing, for this means that God is not all-knowing. The traditional view maintains that God's mind is immovable and thus interprets these texts anthropomorphically—that is, the writers "humanize" God in order to understand God's mysterious actions. In other words, from our finite human perspective, it seems as though God changes God's mind.

Some nontraditional approaches have either rejected or redefined divine all-knowing. Process theology doesn't endorse an all-knowing (or all-powerful) God. Instead, God is all-loving creativity who, like all creation, is still "becoming," still evolving. After all, "I am that I am" can also be translated, "I will be that I will be." As such, the future is unknown, even to God.

Among Evangelicals, there's "open theism". Open theists assert that God is all-knowing: God knows all that exists. But since the future doesn't exist, God doesn't know the future and is "open" to it.

Are we then at the mercy of an unpredictable God? While the Bible affirms both perspectives, two things should be highlighted:

1. When God (seemingly) changes God's mind, it's always on the side of mercy.
2. God never changes God's mind about the promises God made (see Num. 23:19, Isa. 46:10, and Rom. 11:1–2, 29).

## Gary Peluso-Verdend

## Who is...
### Gary Peluso-Verdend

*I wanted to be an astronaut until I learned I needed glasses.*

Yes. In the following answer, I address this specific question rather than the related matter of human beings changing their minds regarding what is in God's mind. But, that said, biblical stories of God changing God's mind are closely, if not umbilically, tied to what human beings do. Even the story of the Great Flood (Gen. 6) is framed as a story of God's regret and action to undo his good creation after human beings had ruined it.

Some stories of God changing God's mind are laced with irony and are more about God's strategy of developing a person's leadership than about God changing God's mind. Take the story of God and Moses in Exodus 32. When Moses was on Mount Sinai receiving the law from God, the people convinced Moses' brother Aaron to create and worship an idol (a golden calf).

God complains to Moses that the people he (Moses) took from Egypt all ought to die. Moses argues why that is a bad idea. God relents, but when Moses goes down the mountain, he assumes the stance toward the people that God had expressed. God "changed God's mind" in order for Moses to assume responsibility.

When we read the prophets—especially Isaiah, Jeremiah, Ezekiel, Micah, and Hosea—we see an "if–then" construction that contains a version of God changing God's mind. The classical prophets in Israel were, as the saying goes, "forth-tellers," not foretellers. They did not predict the future. But they were called by God to speak to the powers of the day regarding idolatry and injustice (a foundational biblical concept). The prophets forth-told the doom that would come if the people continued in their present path; and the good life if they turned from their evil ways.

The important idea here is the prophets believed human actions matter to God. What human beings do affects what God does. God has decided to be vulnerable to human agency. God's mind and actions may change, depending on what we do.

## Scriptural References

Genesis 18:16–33; Exodus 32:1–14; Numbers 23:19; Isaiah 1; Jeremiah 31:27–30; Jonah 3; Mark 7:24–30

## Suggested Additional Sources for Reading

- Karen Armstrong, *A History of God* (Ballantine, 1994).
- Gregory Boyd, *God of the Possible: A Biblical Introduction to the Open View of God* (Baker Books, 2000).
- John B. Cobb Jr. and David Ray Griffin, *Process Theology: An Introductory Exposition* (Westminster/John Knox Press, 1976).
- C. Robert Mesle, *Process Theology: A Basic Introduction* (Chalice Press, 1993).
- Jack Miles, *God: A Biography* (Vintage, 1996).
- Clark Pinnock et al., *The Openness of God: A Biblical Challenge to the Traditional Understanding of God* (IVP Academic, 1994).
- Jerome M. Segal, *Joseph's Bones: Understanding the Struggle between God and Mankind in the Bible* (Riverhead, 2007), especially chap. 4, "The Struggle in the Desert."
- Marjorie Hewitt Suchocki, *God–Christ–Church: A Practical Guide to Process Theology* (Crossroad, 1992).

## Suggested Questions for Further Discussion/Thought

1. What is most unsettling about a God who will change God's mind?
2. What is most comforting about a God who will change God's mind?
3. Do you think much about how "real" God's relationship with us is?
4. What might be at stake if God changes God's mind? Are there any rules of thumb for when God's mind seems open to being changed?

# Does God justify violence in scripture? What about genocide?

## Jarrod McKenna

### Who is...
**Jarrod McKenna**

*I do like walks on the beach (I would mention surfing but it might mislead people into thinking I'm cooler than I really am).*

The Bible doesn't present itself as a collection of refined religious wisdom. The story of God's redemption (the Bible) is as wild, messy and complex as we are. Like Jacob and the angel, what is central to our scriptures is wrestling within the text with God, which climaxes in Christ transfiguring everything through him.

The darkness, horror, and brutality that (miraculously) are not edited out of scripture are nothing other than what God has been wrestling to transform and has done so "in Christ." How our Muslim friends understand their Qur'an is like how we understand the person of Jesus: as the literal Word of God (Jn. 1:14).

If the Bible is authoritative for us (and I hope it is), we must avoid being modern-day Marcionites, editing out (from the Holy Bible or ourselves) that which reveals what God longs to transform. Take the story of genocide in Joshua 11 as an example.

Today, God is no less on the side of oppressed landless minorities fleeing oppressive empires, no less calling us to be a people among them seeking a future of risk against the most powerful military forces in the world, no less a warrior fighting on our behalf. But in Jesus, God has conquered not with a sword, killing his enemies, but with a cross, dying for them (Rev. 12:11). The Bible not only does not justify violence, war, and genocide; in light of Jesus; it abolishes them with the inbreaking of the kingdom.

## Brandon Gilvin

**Who is...**
**Brandon Gilvin**

*I want someday to write an article on 1980s graphic novels, apocalyptic literature, and the end of the Cold War.*

The world has always been a violent place. Some of the earliest stories in the Bible acknowledge this. Whether it's the mythic stories from Genesis, such as Cain's murder of Abel, or the later epic stories that recall violence against women, such as the rape of Tamar, violent acts are part of the stories that make up the Bible. The death of Jesus, which serves as the climax of the gospels, is itself an act of state-sponsored violence (seriously . . . how else would you describe capital punishment?).

Different violent acts are treated differently throughout the Bible. Some acts are punished, others are accepted as collateral damage, and some seem sanctioned.

From my perspective, however, those differences have little to do with how God sees violence. Human beings wrote the stories in the Bible and an invisible, divine hand did not direct them. The people of faith that wrote these stories should be understood as fallible human beings who were struggling to make sense of how God was present in their histories. Sometimes they saw God's presence in the violence waged in their history.

Does this mean that we must see violence in biblical stories as divinely inspired? Does it give us permission to excuse our violence as divinely sanctioned?

Modern readings of the stories in Joshua of the violent conquest of Canaan have been used to justify the slaughter of indigenous people in North America, the apartheid-era violence in South Africa, and the ongoing Israeli-Palestinian conflict. Readings of Paul have been used to justify slavery. Prophetic calls for God's punishment of ancient Israel have been used to excuse the Holocaust.

These are abusive readings. It is inexcusable to justify violence with religion. I suggest an alternative way of approaching the Bible—reading it with the knowledge that those who came before us struggled with the way to find God in every detail of their lives and histories and sometimes got it wrong, and remembering that for every act of violence in the Bible, there is a call to justice and peacemaking, and a story about an individual who suffers an act of violence and cries out.

We as the readers are left to choose what we do with that cry. Do we seek vengeance? or work for reconciliation?

# Gary Peluso-Verdend

One's answer will depend largely on who you think wrote the scriptures. If God is the author and God authorized everything said in God's name, then the answer is yes. However, if you believe human beings authored the scriptures, sometimes inspired by God and sometimes justifying what they wanted to do or had done, then the answer is no. I stand with the latter answer.

There are scores of references to doing violence in God's name, with several justifying reasons. If people are being attacked, they might pray for strength against their enemies (self-defense). When the newly forming people of Israel approached Canaan at the end of their desert wanderings, they began their assaults on the people of the land believing (or writing later to justify their actions) that God had given them the land (conquest). In Elijah's infamous contest with the prophets of Baal, God's prophet exterminated the false prophets (purification), who promoted a polluting religion in the land.

Examples of violence in God's name are evident in the New Testament, too, but the examples differ from the Old Testament period. In the New Testament period, Israel lived as a client state of the Roman Empire and, as such, did not have to wrestle with questions of national defense as it did during the years between David's reign (about 1000 B.C.E.) and the Babylonian captivity (sixth century B.C.E.).

In first-century C.E. Palestine, some Jewish guerilla groups (Zealots) took action into their own hands and struck Roman targets directly. Others prayed and dreamed of the day when Rome would be overthrown and God's reign would be established; this is the theme running through the book of Revelation.

No, God does not justify violence or genocide through the scriptures, but human authors do.

## Scriptural References

Genesis 6:5–7; 2 Samuel 13; Micah 6:8; Isaiah 11; Joshua 10, 11; 1 Kings 18:20–40; Mark 13; John 1:14; 14:6; Philemon; Hebrews 12:2; Colossians 1:15

## Suggested Additional Sources for Reading

- Dave Andrews, *Plan Be* (published by the author).
- Walter Brueggemann, *Divine Presence amid Violence: Contextualizing the Book of Joshua* (Cascade, 2009).
- Lee C. Camp, *Mere Discipleship: Radical Christianity in a Rebellious World* (Brazos, 2008).
- C. S. Cowles, *Show Them No Mercy* (Zondervan, 2003).
- Phyllis Tribble, *Texts of Terror: Literary-Feminist Readings of Biblical Narratives* (Fortress Press, 1984).
- James G. Williams, ed., *The Rene Girard Reader* (Crossroad, 1996).
- Walter Wink, *Engaging the Powers: Discernment and Resistance in an Age of Domination* (Fortress Press, 1992).

## Suggested Questions for Further Discussion/Thought

1. How does the violence in the scriptures reveal the violence in ourselves?
2. What would it look like to not "edit out" this violence but let God transform it in Christ?
3. Do you see scriptures still used today to justify violence? How so?
4. How does Jesus' call to nonviolence "perfect" the ancient laws that preceded him?

# Why is the gospel of John so different from the other three gospels?

## David J. Lose

### Who is...
**David J. Lose**

*I love almost anything that combines peanut butter and chocolate.*

---

Matthew, Mark, and Luke are like siblings—while they may have distinct features and different temperaments, they still look a lot alike. John, on the other hand, is more like a distant cousin. He knows a few stories about Jesus like those in the other gospels, but largely relies on other material. Why? John was probably writing to a different early Christian community with different questions and concerns.

It seems likely that John's community was made up of Jewish followers of Jesus who had been kicked out of their synagogue for their beliefs. John therefore encourages his listeners to believe in Jesus even if they suffer persecution. John explains how and why Jesus really is the Jewish messiah, and so regularly points out how what happens to Jesus fulfills the scriptures.

Similarly, John regularly names as "signs" what we would call miracles—they are clues to Jesus' identity. After each sign, Jesus usually makes a long speech using different images (vine, light, good shepherd, bread, etc.) to describe who he is. In John's gospel, Jesus is both confident (he knows he is doing his Father's work) and powerful (he seems hardly to suffer during his crucifixion) and so serves as an example to John's audience.

Jesus also tells his disciples that he is going away, that they will be persecuted, and that he will send them help in the form of the Holy Spirit, all of which was undoubtedly comforting to John's outcast community.

John, at heart, is less a historian or a storyteller than he is a theologian. (The symbol for John is the eagle because, according to St. Augustine, his theology soars above the other gospels.) John very much wants his audience to understand the theological significance of Jesus as the Jewish Messiah and to believe in him.

## Jarrod McKenna

John's gospel was written last. While some think this makes it less potent, I think the opposite is true (as did radical Christian groups like the early Quakers, who quoted it more than any other book). The gospel of John has had longer to ferment and the imagery and archetypes of the book are infused with what is fully revealed in the Incarnation, in a way that is significantly different from the other gospels. In John, Jesus is more than teacher; Jesus is the revealer! John insists: Jesus is the judgment (Jn. 3:19). Jesus is God's future now (Jn. 11:25). Jesus is God (Jn. 10:30).

It's for this reason that many have considered the apostle John to be the first Christian mystic, who presents us with the risen victorious victim of the system, redeeming all of creation. In the gospel of John, God has moved into the neighborhood (Jn. 1:14), taking the system (and its survival on the sacrifice of the weak) down from the inside. In John's gospel, Jesus warns that if we don't read the whole Bible through his life, we will study the scriptures "day and night" yet still miss the life that God longs to give us (Jn. 5:39–40).

Jesus' continual "I Am" statements confront us with the reality that Christ not only saves us from our sin, but also in a sense saves God from our projections of violence and injustice. John's gospel demands that any images of God that do not look like a love that would wash the feet of an enemy who would betray you (Jn. 13:15) be radically abandoned.

## José F. Morales Jr.

Probably the best way to answer this is by first asking why Matthew, Mark, and Luke are so similar.

Academic consensus says that Mark was written first. Also, scholars overwhelmingly agree that Matthew and Luke had copies of Mark's gospel when they were writing their versions. But as they wrote, they copied large chunks of Mark when writing their versions. (Back then, it was OK to do that. Now, it's plagiarism!) John didn't copy Mark.

This is not to say that Matthew and Luke are simply "extra-strength" Mark. They reworked parts of what they used and added their own stuff. Each of the three had a different portrayal of Jesus of Nazareth that they depicted in their respective renditions.

John doesn't borrow from Mark and therefore is substantially different from the other three, though it should be noted that John's gospel does have much in common with them as well—for example, Jesus' baptism, feeding the multitude, and the crucifixion.

Also, each writer had a different theological agenda for his writing, and this shaped his telling of the story of Jesus. The evangelists were less concerned with writing an accurate historical account of the human Jesus. Rather, as Garry Wills, author of *What Jesus Meant,* points out, they were trying to answer this question: What does Jesus mean for us?

## Joshua Toulouse

### Who is...
#### Joshua Toulouse

*I believe every year that this will be the year the Cubs win the World Series. (Go Cubs!)*

While it's believed the gospel of John was written later than Mark, Matthew, or Luke, scholars also believe that the author of John didn't use, or perhaps didn't even know of, the other gospels. Consensus these days is that Mark was written first among the four gospels and then was used as a source in the writing of Matthew and Luke.

Matthew and Luke are then also believed to have used another common source (generally referred to as "Q," short for *quelle,* which means source) as well as sources specific to themselves (referred to as "M" for Matthew and "L" for Luke).

If John was written without using (or perhaps even being aware) of any of these sources, we could certainly expect that it would be different in its composition. And just as Mark, Matthew, and Luke were written for different audiences in different situations with different needs, so too was John. Some of the theological decisions concerning John's understanding and description of Jesus help explain some of the differences.

For instance, while the other three gospels have Jesus baptized, John does not have an explicit baptism scene. In the other three gospels, this scene serves as a legitimation of Jesus' ministry, but John opens with Jesus being with God and of God, legitimized before he is even born. This makes the birth and baptism stories less necessary.

## Scriptural References

Mark 1: 9–11, 14–15, 35–39; 3:13–17; Luke 3:21–22; 4:14–21; John 1:1–5; 3:22–36; 9—10; 20:30–31

## Suggested Additional Sources for Reading

- James Alison, *Living in the End Times* (SPCK, 1997).
- Marcus J. Borg and N. T. Wright, *The Meaning of Jesus: Two Visions* (HarperOne, 2007).
- Raymond Brown, *The Community of the Beloved Disciple: The Life, Loves, and Hates of an Individual Church in New Testament Times* (Paulist Press, 1978).
- Warren Carter, *John: Storyteller, Interpreter, Evangelist* (Hendrickson, 2006).
- Richard B. Hays, *The Moral Vision of the New Testament* (HarperOne, 1996).
- Craig Koester, *The Word of Life: A Theology of John's Gospel* (Eerdmans, 2008).
- Robert Kysar, *John, the Maverick Gospel,* 3d edition (Westminster John Knox Press, 2007).
- Mark Allen Powell, *Fortress Introduction to the Gospels* (Fortress Press, 1998).
- Garry Wills, *What Jesus Meant* (Penguin, 2007).
- Garry Wills, *What the Gospels Meant* (Viking, 2008).

## Suggested Questions for Further Discussion/Thought

1. Which image of Jesus in John's gospel do you find most helpful in understanding his identity and mission?
2. Jarrod suggests that any images of God that don't look like Jesus' actions in John 13 must be abandoned. Do you have ideas about God that don't look like Jesus' love?
3. Compare the judgment images of Matthew 25 with John 3's insistence that Jesus is the judgment. How do you understand these passages together?
4. Dietrich Bonhoeffer, the twentieth-century theologian and martyr who died at the hands of the Nazis, once said that a Christian is one who every day answers Jesus' question, "Who do you say I am?" So who do you say Jesus is? What does Jesus mean for you?
5. Read Mark 1:14–15, 35–39; Luke 4:14–21; and John 3:16–18 and 10:14–18. According to each evangelist, why did Jesus come? What was his purpose?

*Hell, Sheol, Hades, Gehenna, and Tartarus are all labeled as "hell" by most Christians. Are they really the same? Are they all places of fiery torment? Are such things to be taken literally, metaphorically, or as myth?*

## David J. Lose

These places aren't all the same, but they're similar enough that you can understand why people lump them together. In brief, "Sheol" and "Hades" represent the realm of the dead, the place where both good and bad people go after death. "Gehenna" and "Tartarus," on the other hand, are reserved for wicked people and are places of punishment. Hell, a word that comes from Old English, has become a catch-all phrase for the others, but for the last two especially.

On the whole, the Bible doesn't talk a whole lot about any of these places and so I'm a little leery of giving them much significance in our own theology. I get downright suspicious of folks that seem to like talking about eternal punishment, as that seems out of sync with Jesus' emphasis on God's love.

Too often in the church's history, hell has been used to scare people into doing what the church wants them to. For this reason, some people think we've outgrown the usefulness of concepts like hell and damnation. Others, however, would argue that we wouldn't appreciate heaven without the threat of hell.

Insofar as hell depicts ultimate separation from God, I tend to think that whether it's an actual physical place or a metaphor, it's a good place to avoid. On that score, I take hope from the apostle Paul's declaration that "neither death, nor life, nor angels, nor rulers, nor things present, nor things to come, nor powers, nor height, nor depth, nor anything else in all creation will be able to separate us from the love of God in Christ Jesus our Lord" (Rom. 8:38–39). Sounds good to me.

## Gary Peluso-Verdend

No, the meaning of these words is not the same. Rather, we have different symbols from different symbol systems.

"Sheol" is a Hebrew word, found in the pre-sixth-century-B.C.E. portions of the Old Testament. Ancient Judaism did not conceive of human beings as part body and part soul. Rather, human beings were understood as flesh animated by the breath of God. Whatever existence a person had after death was thought to be in a place called Sheol, a place of shades, where there is no consciousness. Sheol contains neither pleasures nor torments.

During Israel's captivity in Babylon, Jews were exposed to Zoroastrianism, a religion that includes a belief in resurrection and a two-place afterlife—the equivalent of heaven and hell. By New Testament times, belief in resurrection, heaven, and hell were widespread—albeit not universal—in Judaism.

Hell as a place of torment and stink became well developed many centuries after the Bible by the Christian writer Dante Alighieri, but sometimes the roots of a mythical or nonphysical place are found in real places. "Gehenna," as a place of torment for evil people, was associated with the Valley of Hinnom, south of Jerusalem, where the city dumped its garbage.

Very important beliefs are associated with hell, such as sin, judgment, consequence, and resurrection. Christianity—or any other religion—is like a language; one must understand each symbol within a greater grammar.

## Jason Boyett

### Who is...
### Jason Boyett

*I can recite the alphabet faster in reverse than I can say it in alphabetical order.*

No, they are not the same. Four words—the Hebrew word "Sheol" and the Greek words "Hades," "Gehenna," and "Tartarus"—have been translated as the English word hell. We think of hell as a fiery place of torment for sinners, but only "Gehenna" fits that description.

Sheol was an all-purpose term referring to the shadowy realm of the dead (the grave), and earlier Old Testament books seem to indicate that everyone goes there—not just the wicked. In the New Testament, the Greek word Hades is used interchangeably with Sheol—it's the place of the dead. Tartarus appears only once in the Bible, in 2 Peter 2:4. It refers to Tartarus, the dungeon-like netherworld in Greek mythology filled with suffering and torment. The context indicates it is where demons reside.

The hell-as-torture-chamber idea comes from Gehenna, which Jesus described as a destination for sinners. This word originates with a Hebrew name, Ge-Hinnom, which refers to the Hinnom Valley, a garbage dump outside Jerusalem. Trash, animal carcasses, and the bodies of criminals were dumped there, and the valley burned continuously—an evocative image of hell.

Do we take the idea of a burning hell literally? Jesus certainly spoke as if it were a real place. But keep in mind that the idea of a dualistic afterlife—a hell for sinners and heaven for the righteous—was a relatively new idea to Judaism, possibly due to the influence of Zoroastrianism during the Babylonian exile. It was a theological departure from the ancient faith of the Jewish patriarchs.

# Craig Detweiler

While death is a certain fact, it is also prompts an air of mystery. What happens when our hearts stop beating? Is there something on the other side of life? Descriptions of hell (and heaven) are all rather speculative, more poetic than precise.

The Hebrew word "Sheol" describes the grave that awaits us all. It is a shadowy place, something we've all glimpsed at a funeral but never experienced from the inside. Our bodies are all bound for Sheol, irrespective of our beliefs or practices. None escape physical death.

When the Hebrew scriptures were translated into the Greek language, the word "Hades" was chosen to describe the ground or pit our bodies are bound for. The Greek notion of Hades was more of a shady, mythological place than a physical grave.

Within Greek mythology, Tartarus is a place of judgment and torment, a pit much farther down than the more benign Hades. Only once does the word Tartarus appear in scripture. In 2 Peter 2:4, God punishes sinful angels by throwing them into Tartarus, a dark pit reserved for judgment.

When the Bible was translated into English, Hades and Sheol were translated as hell. Unfortunately, such a reference comes across as much more loaded than "the grave." It had eternal associations rather than a tangible, temporal, or physical meaning.

The associations of hell with a fire, torment, and eternal anonymity start coming into play with a term like "Gehenna." It is a destination we would all want to avoid. It is a place where people who lack family, resources, and significance are discarded. No one wants to feel so unloved, unacknowledged, or unnoticed.

## Scriptural References

Genesis 37:35; Deuteronomy; 32:22 (Sheol); Psalm 6:5; Romans 8:38–39; Matthew 5:22 (Gehenna) and 16:18 (Hades); 2 Peter 2:4 (Tartarus); 1 John 4:7; Revelation 20:10

## Suggested Additional Sources for Reading

- Jason Boyett, *Pocket Guide to the Afterlife* (Jossey-Bass, 2009).
- Stanley N. Gundry et al., *Four Views of Hell* (Zondervan, 1997).
- Alice K. Turner, *The History of Hell* (Mariner, 1995).
- T. J. Wray and Gregory Mobley, *The Birth of Satan: Tracing the Devil's Biblical Roots* (Palgrave Macmillan, 2005).

## Suggested Questions for Further Discussion/Thought

1. Why is hell such an important concept to some Christians?
2. What do our beliefs about hell say about our theology, or picture, of God?
3. Most Christians believe in a dualistic afterlife (heaven and hell). Yet a fiery place of torment is in contrast to the idea of Sheol as found in most of the Old Testament. Still, Jesus clearly believes in a fiery hell. Is this a doctrine that "evolved" from the Old Testament to the New Testament? How do you reconcile two contrasting doctrines if both have biblical support?

## Are there secret codes embedded in scripture? What are they?

### David J. Lose

No. Really. Then why all the speculation about secret codes, symbols, and keys that unlock everything from the true meaning of the Bible to a blueprint for the end of the world?

First, the Bible is admittedly a complicated book. What we pick up and read is the end result of centuries of writing, rewriting, collecting, and editing of all kinds of different literary genres from a number of different cultures and historical eras. It is, at many points, a tough read. Little wonder, then, that we wish for a hidden code that could make transparent what sometimes feels fairly obscure.

But there's a second, more basic reason: Human beings are essentially insecure creatures. That is, we have no way of determining our own worth, value, or standing in the universe, and so we all too often compare ourselves—both favorably and unfavorably—to those around us. It's not a pretty picture, but look around and see how often we use things like gender, economic class, education, race, and ethnicity to establish various pecking orders.

One way that people have compared themselves—almost always favorably—to others is by trying to demonstrate that they are smarter than the ordinary schmucks around them. Purporting a kind of mysterious or secret knowledge, some readers of scripture have claimed to be able to penetrate the pages of the Bible to unravel humanity's deepest secrets, secrets that are unavailable to the masses (which includes you and me).

Don't believe it. The Bible can be challenging, but if you take your time to read it carefully, not only will you be able to understand, but you'll also come across the only antidote to human insecurity—God's unconditional promise of love and acceptance for us just as we are.

## Christian Piatt

**Who is...**
### Christian Piatt

*The tendon in my left pinky finger is too short,
which makes my finger permanently crooked.*

There are countless theories about secret codes embedded in texts of the Bible, but the best known is the Kabbalistic—or ancient mystical Jewish—belief that the true name of God is embedded in the book of Exodus, specifically in Exodus 2:18 through 3:7.

As I wrote in my book *Lost: A Search for Meaning,* God's name according to Kabbalah "is represented by the letters 'YHVH,' generally pronounced 'Yahweh,' or 'Yahveh.' The Hebrew word 'Adonai' is used as a reference to God in scripture, but it is not actually the name of God."

Kabbalah teaches that God's name actually is 216 letters long and is embedded in the book of Exodus as a code. There are three verses in Exodus 14:19–21, each of which is seventy-two letters in length. By combining the letters in certain patterns, an algorithm is developed that is the key to knowing God's true name.

Not to be mistaken for this interpretation of sacred texts is another ancient Jewish practice of interpretation called "midrash." Still practiced today by many religious scholars, preachers, and even laity in the Jewish and Christian faiths, midrash does not focus on embedded codes but, rather, helps guide readers through the process of revealing multiple meanings within a single text. These may include literal, historic/cultural, mystical, and other interpretations, and often times no single interpretation is considered the "right" one.

Though humanity seems obsessed with deciphering hidden meaning nearly anywhere we can find it, a point is well-taken from Jesus when he is asked about the end of the world. His response, to paraphrase, is that no one, including him, knows when such things will take place. Further, it's not our business to waste energy worrying about it.

### Scriptural References

Exodus 2:18—3:7; 14:19–21

## Suggested Additional Sources for Reading

- Darren Aronofsky, *Pi: Faith in Chaos*, film.
- Thomas Inman and John Newton, *Ancient Pagan and Modern Christian Symbolism* (Nabu Press, 2010).
- Daniel C. Matt, *The Essential Kabbalah: The Heart of Jewish Mysticism* (HarperOne, 1996).
- Christian Piatt, *Lost: A Search for Meaning* (Chalice Press, 2006).

## Suggested Questions for Further Discussion/Thought

1. Why do you think scriptures suggest that human beings cannot speak the name of God? And why are some so intent on speaking it anyway?
2. Are there any passages in the Bible that seem cryptic to you, or possibly allude to some other hidden meaning? Like what?
3. Watch the movie *Pi*. What sort of power do people, both in the film and in real life, give to things they don't really understand? Why? Can this be dangerous?

# Question

*How can we begin to take the Bible literally when it seems to contradict itself so often?*

## Rebecca Bowman Woods

### Who is...
**Rebecca Bowman Woods**

*If I could live anywhere, I'd choose the Florida Keys.*

During my ordination interviews, I was asked my views on the Bible's authorship. My response: While the Bible is sacred scripture, humanity's grubby fingerprints are all over it. Fortunately, the committee liked my answer.

This may seem like a paradox, but for me it's easier to take the Bible seriously by viewing it as a joint venture between God and people rather than picturing God dictating every word and expecting us to read it literally.

Contradictions arise because people wrote it with different theological perspectives across a period of hundreds of years. Some authors tell the same stories again, in different ways. For example, the history of Israel in 1 and 2 Samuel and 1 and 2 Kings is retold in 1 and 2 Chronicles by an author who changed some of the specifics to convey his own views and to answer questions of his own era.

The four gospels tell of Jesus' earthly ministry but the events aren't in the same sequence, and when the gospel writers include the same story, the details are off. And the apostle Paul of the book of Acts is not the same Paul who emerges from reading his letters.

People try to harmonize or overlook these differences, but to the inquisitive reader, they are valuable clues about the authors and their situations. Yes, the biblical authors (and some of the copyists who added to and subtracted from the manuscripts) had agendas, biases, and perspectives, just as all of us do.

Even though biblical stories differ, what the tellers and authors had in common was the experience of God—through personal encounters and the sacred teachings, writings, and traditions of faith communities.

## Gary Peluso-Verdend

Better not to begin to take the Bible literally! Rather, take it seriously and learn to interpret it.

What does it mean to take the Bible literally? Most if not all of the Bible circulated orally at first, sometimes for generations. The transformation from oral to written text occurred in different time periods. By way of various scribes in different places, using varying texts that sometimes contradicted other texts in significant ways, the oral became written.

A variety of literary forms is evident in the Bible: narrative, allegory, parable, poetry, fiction, historical records, reports of fantastical ecstatic experiences, metaphor, and myth (which does not mean "untrue," but is an ahistorical means to express something that is true at the deepest levels). Most of these poetic and literary forms cannot be interpreted literally.

The Bible should be read only in context. The context for reading the Bible will include the historical context and our contemporary context. Responsible readers will seek to be informed by scholarship regarding what the text meant, and they will read the text today with a community of readers that will help keep any reading as honest as possible.

Are there contradictions in the Bible? Yes. Many voices are expressed through the Bible. Think of the Bible as a partial record of the experiences, conversations, and debates of the people of God over time. We are privileged to overhear the conversations and debates embedded in this living document!

It would be a mistake to stifle, repress, or resolve all of the debates and contradictions of contemporary Christianity. Shutting down the debates and resolving the contradictions of the text would diminish the power of the Bible. God speaks with one voice but humankind listens with many ears!

## Kathy Escobar

### Who is...
#### Kathy Escobar

*I birthed all five of my children with no pain medication.*

When I became a Christian, I immersed myself in the Bible and in extremely conservative evangelical churches that elevated the Bible to the nth degree. I love the Bible. It is a beautiful, challenging, and supernatural book; its words are "sharper than any two-edged sword" (Heb. 4:12).

One thing that has helped me the most over the past years in letting go of Bible worship and assuming that "if you don't take it literally then the whole thing falls apart" is remembering that interpretation of the Bible is varied.

Years ago, a very strict Calvinist friend of mine took a course in biblical counseling. She was dismissing the counseling degree I'd started to pursue at seminary, saying that it was not "biblical enough." I remember heated conversations with her in which I reminded her that her course was merely the instructor's interpretation and application of the Bible. In the same vein, we need to get more honest about that when it comes to literal interpretation.

Each person who "interprets" the Bible can do that work through extensive exegesis, commentaries, and a wide variety of other research, but it is still filtered through that person's lens. It's presumptuous of anyone to think he or she has the market cornered on exactly what God meant. The Bible is just too complicated for that, and there are too many contradictions that can't be completely answered.

As a pastor, I always tell people, "This is just my take on this passage; I am sure there are others who see it differently." I think we need to be more honest about "literal interpretation" and admit that if we really took the Bible literally, most of our churches wouldn't look the way they look, and we wouldn't wear what we wear or care about the things we care about. Many are good at "selective literal interpretation," choosing to align with some passages and completely dismiss others.

I think I am becoming more honest about the inability to reconcile completely the inconsistencies in the Bible. Like so many other issues of faith, intellectualizing them doesn't always work, no matter how hard we try to make sense of it.

## Joshua Einsohn

### Who is...
**Joshua Einsohn**

*I have met some of the most wonderful, creative, giving people in the world in an industry that is generally considered shallow and superficial (entertainment).*

A strict, literal interpretation of the Bible is so fraught with potential contradiction that it should be avoided at all costs to prevent either a great deal of teeth gnashing (and expensive dental work) or a slowly numbing lack of critical thought.

In college, I was often in classes with a certain poor girl who was a fundamentalist Christian and believed the literal word of the Bible. Incidentally, I don't consider her to be a "poor girl" because she was a fundamentalist Christian! I felt sorry for her because she kept taking classes that frequently rendered her distraught. Here's how class went pretty much every day for "Jane."

*Classmate*: If the total population of the world was Adam, Eve, Cain, and Abel, and Abel smote Cain and then had the "mark of Cain" put on his forehead so that all the rest of the people of the world would know the awful thing he did, who are the rest of the people? Mom and Dad?
*Jane*: (confidently) No, the heathens.
*Classmate*: It doesn't say anything about God creating heathens.
*Jane*: (less confidently) Yes it did . . . when he created the beasts.
*Classmate*: Did you just call all the non-Christians "beasts"?
*Jane*: (tearing up) Well . . . yes . . .

At this point, the class erupted and she burst into tears. In every class I had with her, the waterworks would start up at least once a week. Her superior critical thinking continually butted up against her literal belief in the Bible. The interesting thing was that she could easily have made it through college without taking those courses, and yet she kept signing up for them. I've always wondered if she managed to reconcile the two sides of herself.

## Scriptural References

Genesis 1, 2; Matthew 1:18—2:23; 5:21–48; Luke 2:1–20; Hebrews 4

## Suggested Additional Sources for Reading

- Karen Armstrong, *The Battle for God* (Ballantine, 2001).
- Marcus J. Borg, *Reading the Bible again for the First Time: Taking the Bible Seriously but Not Literally* (Harper San Francisco, 2002).

## Suggested Questions for Further Discussion/Thought

1. Do you think it's possible to take parts of the Bible literally and leave out others?
2. Does fixating on literal interpretation limit God?
3. How are you learning to live with the inconsistencies in the Bible? What does that look like, feel like, for you?
4. Can two statements that seem to contradict each other somehow both be true? If so, how?

*If I don't believe every word of the Bible is literally true, how do I know what to consider in context and what to set aside?*

## Gary Peluso-Verdend

**Who is...**
### Gary Peluso-Verdend

*I have never smoked—anything, ever.*

This is one of the most important questions anyone or any community can bring to the Bible. In Proverbs 1:7 we read, "The fear of the Lord is the beginning of knowledge." Another beginning of knowledge is the realization that the Bible does not say anything but is one part of a two-party communication. There is the Bible and there is the interpreter. No one, and no community, listens without interpreting.

This claim regarding interpretation begs a question regarding we who interpret: In which circle of interpreters will we stand? While the printing press (and now iPhones and Kindles) allows us to read the Bible individually, one should not read the Bible only alone. Everyone who reads the Bible needs to choose the companions with whom he or she will read—which interpreters, from which centuries, with which theological perspective(s), representing which communities, from which countries, addressing which audiences?

It is also the case that the Bible contains many different kinds of literature, including historical narrative, moral codes, visions, poetry, parables, extended metaphors, and more. No one of these kinds of literature can be interpreted responsibly without inquiring into the context within which a particular slice of scripture should be interpreted.

Our circles of interpreters are companions and guides in rendering the weighty judgments regarding what is the Word of God, or the words of God, or the words that some community at some time thought God was saying but that we now consider to be the words of fallible human beings.

## Nadia Bolz-Weber

### Who is...
### Nadia Bolz-Weber

*The first album I bought was The Ramones'*
Road to Ruin *(I was twelve).*

The books in what we now call the Bible are known as the canon, although it is important to note that there is more than one canon. Our Roman Catholic and Orthodox brothers and sisters have a slightly different set of books in their Bibles. We Lutherans believe there to be what we call a "canon within the canon." In other words, there are some parts of the Bible that are central and some that are peripheral.

To us, the gospel is the canon within the canon. Luther spoke of the Bible as the cradle that holds Christ. The Bible is not Christ; the Bible bears witness to Christ and the good news of the new thing done in Christ's birth, life, death, and resurrection. This is the central message of the Bible and the lens through which it is read. Therefore, the parts of the Bible that do not hold up against the gospel simply do not have the same authority.

There are many messages one can hear from the biblical text. A case could be made that God hates lobsters and crabs based on Leviticus 11:9–12. The Bible contains enough writings that one could make a case for just about anything.

But what is the central message? Christ.

## José F. Morales Jr.

### Who is...
### José F. Morales Jr.

*I'm a morning person and a night owl, which means
that around 3 p.m., I'm completely useless.*

We don't "set aside" any part of the Bible.

Martin Copenhaver and Anthony Robinson decided to write letters to their teenage kids about God, the church, and other things, and to give these letters to their kids as they prepared to go to college. One of the letters, compiled in their book *Words for the Journey*, dealt with the parts of the Bible that are difficult to understand or accept.

In the letter, the authors use the analogy of a filing system. They said that the parts they accept are stowed away in the file drawer. The parts that are difficult or those they can't stand (e.g., killing babies in Psalm 137), they do not throw away. Rather, they leave them on the desk, right in front of them—forced to wrestle with them again and again. We fight with hard texts; we don't dismiss them even if we hate them.

In his fabulous *The Good Book,* Peter Gomes asserts that even though the Bible doesn't change, we do. Our "culture of interpretation," which shapes the way we read and react to scripture, changes. At some point in human history, the images of God as warrior were comforting for folks, not necessarily because they were blood-hungry killers but because within their context, Warrior God made sense. Today, with all the unnecessary wars and the equally unnecessary weapons of mass destruction, God as "general" may not serve us well.

Instead of "setting aside," ask what the core of the biblical story is. Scripture itself helps us. If we take note of the events that are repeatedly mentioned and reflected upon throughout the Bible, we find there are two: the Exodus and Christ. In both, God liberates and we faithfully respond by joining God in that liberating process. I say, begin there.

## Rebecca Bowman Woods

You don't need to be a biblical scholar to read the Bible nonliterally and interpret it wisely. You just need to ask questions. Reading the Bible critically—acknowledging your questions about the text—doesn't mean you're criticizing the Bible or God. After all, God gave us the gift of intellect and the capacity to learn. Would God expect us to put these aside when approaching the Bible?

Take the parable of the mustard seed in Luke 13:18–19. Jesus compares the kingdom of God to "a mustard seed that someone took and sowed in the garden; it grew and became a tree, and the birds of the air made nests in its branches." Most people assume that the comparison is favorable. Jesus wouldn't compare God's realm to something odd or ordinary, would he?

Read the text slowly, and consult more than one translation if you can. Make a list of questions, such as the following:

- Where is Jesus, and to whom is he speaking?
- Would a mustard plant have been considered useful? Beautiful? Common?
- Would it normally be planted in a garden?
- What about the birds? Would their presence be welcomed or not?
- Were any objects in the story—mustard seed, tree, garden, birds, branches—common symbols for something else?
- Is this parable in any other gospels? How are those versions different?

A good study Bible will answer some questions. You can do research on the Internet or at a public, university, or seminary library. Over time, you'll discover which sources are resources are the most credible and useful.

Your questions are the road map for your investigation of the text. Some will lead to dead ends, but others will take you to surprising places.

## Joshua Toulouse

### Who is...
### Joshua Toulouse

*I always completely make up a lie for Fact Number Four when asked to come up with five facts about myself.*

Everything in the Bible is considered as scripture, so we shouldn't just ignore what we don't like, although there are plenty of people who do just that. To decide how to interpret any part of the Bible, it's important to know the context of what you are reading. While you can, and will, interpret the Bible based on your current context, understanding what the original author intended and how the original audience understood it will only help make modern interpretations easier.

It is also important to remember to be open to God in the reading of scripture, because, while you might not believe that the Bible is the literal word of God handed down, you can believe that the Bible was inspired by God—that God was active in those who wrote it and is still active in your hearing and reading of it today.

### Scriptural References

Deuteronomy 21:18–21; Song of Songs; Psalm 135, 136; Luke 13:18–19; 15:11–32; 1 Corinthians 15:1–8; Revelation 1:1–3

### Suggested Additional Sources for Reading

- Bible Gateway: http://www.biblegateway.com.
- Marcus J. Borg, *The Heart of Christianity: Rediscovering a Life of Faith* (HarperOne, 2003), especially chap. 3, "The Bible: The Heart of the Tradition."
- Marcus J. Borg, *Reading the Bible again for the First Time: Taking the Bible Seriously but Not Literally* (Harper San Francisco, 2002).

- John J. Collins, *A Short Introduction to the Hebrew Bible* (Fortress Press, 2007).
- Martin Copenhaver and Anthony Robinson, *Words for the Journey: Letters to Our Teenagers about Life and Faith* (Pilgrim Press, 2003), especially chap. 18, "The Really Hard Parts of the Bible."
- Peter J. Gomes, *The Good Book: Reading the Bible with Mind and Heart* (HarperOne, 2002), especially chap. 2, "A Matter of Interpretation" and chap. 6, "The Bible and Anti-Semitism: Christianity's Original Sin."
- Luke Timothy Johnson, *The Writings of the New Testament: An Interpretation* (Fortress Press, 2002).
- Textweek: http://www.textweek.com.

## Suggested Questions for Further Discussion/Thought

1. Read 1 Corinthians 15:1–8. In this passage, Paul gives us what, in his opinion, is the "core" of the gospel. Do you agree with him? If so, why? If not, what would you say is the core of the gospel?
2. José Morales suggests that the core events of the biblical story are the Exodus and Christ. Do you agree with him? Why? If not, what are the "core" events of the Bible?
3. Do you believe it's possible to read the Bible literally? Why or why not?
4. Besides a literal reading, what are some other ways of reading and interpreting the Bible?
5. If Bible commentaries were written in the 1700s, 1800s, or early 1900s, are they still useful? What about free Bible commentaries on the Web?

*In the Old Testament, God seems to be actively involved in world events. In the New Testament, God is portrayed as less interventionist but still directly involved. Now, it seems God is much more abstract. What happened, and is this a good or a bad thing?*

### Gary Peluso-Verdend

Nothing happened to God, fundamentally. What happened is that the biblical writers reflect two different eras, and today we read the text and think about God from yet another point of view.

The Christian Old Testament (note: The books of the Hebrew Bible are arranged in a different order from the Old Testament) begins with God's creation of the world and then a series of covenants that God makes with a chosen people. Much of the remainder of the Old Testament is the stories of how those covenants worked out in history—or at least how those who wrote the history remembered it.

The writers consistently understand God to be the God of Abraham, Isaac, and Jacob. The story of God is told through the lenses of God's interactions with God's chosen people. God forms God's people into a nation and gives them land—land that was inhabited by other peoples and that sits at the crossroads of empires, meaning that from Israel's perspective, there was a lot for God to do!

In the New Testament period, Israel no longer exists, Palestine is a client state of the Roman Empire, and most of the New Testament writers reflect a view of God who, for whatever reason, is allowing a time of Roman oppression that God will bring to an end—perhaps soon, perhaps through a messiah. But the worldview of a God who acts in history for the sake of God's people is relatively the same.

God has not withdrawn from history. The lenses of biblical times are no longer the dominant ones, at least in the West. We've added powerful new perspectives to our worldview. Views formed by physics, astronomy, biology, brain studies, sociology, anthropology, and psychology complicate how we think about human agency and how we think about God's agency. And the relationship between God's agency and human agency is one of the most important understandings expressed in any religion.

## Jarrod McKenna

**Who is...**
**Jarrod McKenna**

*Marx Brothers films are underrated.*

A. This question reveals two worldviews that bastardize the gospel, giving birth to cheap imitations. And as Ammon Hennacy reminded us, "When choosing the lesser of two evils we must not forget they are both evil." The two evils are the following:

1. *God is elsewhere.* This would explain the amount of evil, injustice, misery, and war in the world. God created all, but took some time off afterward, holidaying somewhere nicer, maybe by a celestial pool, while we suffer. The founders of the United States believed in a form of this called Deism. In this worldview, Jesus might be the deity popping back, seeing everything has gone to crap and then saying, "Believe in me and I'll take you elsewhere, too." The early church called this heresy "gnosticism." In this worldview, God is abstract because God is a secret "get-out-of-creation-free" card.

The other popular option that equally lacks the revolutionary energy and impulse of the scriptures is that God is not far off because:

2. *God is everything.* Now, if you've grown up in a worldview in which God is always absent, where spirituality has nothing to do with creation, and where your body was always seen as bad, this might sound like a better option. Sometimes called "pantheism," it leaves us with no cosmic critique of the evil of injustice while affirming the goodness and sacredness of creation. Wars, empires, and violence in creation are all just a part of "God/Gaia/the Divine." Jesus just shows up to "enlighten us."

*God is redeemer* is the biblical vision that, in nuanced and elegant ways, radically affirms the goodness of the web of creation while providing an equally radical critique of all violence and injustice that has colonized it as an alien force. As Creating, Sustaining and Redeeming, the Trinity is dynamically involved in history and has acted decisively in the Incarnation, to heal the brokenness we all know, with the wholeness we sometimes feel. This will not leave us with "abstract ideas" but with an invitation to action, for by grace we can be part of God's "intervention" of the Kingdom.

## Scriptural References

Genesis 1, 11; Acts 1:6–7

## Suggested Additional Sources for Reading

- Rita Nakashima Brock and Rebecca Ann Parker, *Saving Paradise: How Christianity Traded Love of This World for Crucifixion and Empire* (Beacon, 2009).
- Lee C. Camp, *Mere Discipleship: Radical Christianity in a Rebellious World* (Brazos, 2008).
- Richard A. Horsley, *Jesus and Empire: The Kingdom of God and the New World Disorder* (Fortress Press, 2002).
- N. T. Wright, *Simply Christian: Why Christianity Makes Sense* (HarperOne, 2010).

## Suggested Questions for Further Discussion/Thought

1. How have you been taught to think of God as elsewhere or everything? How do these understandings of God affect your ideas about suffering or injustice?
2. How might the kingdom "invitation to action" that Jarrod talked about help us feel like God is not so abstract?
3. Take the God Image survey at the end of this book. What is your God Image based on this? Do the results surprise you? With which contributors do your results match best? Do you tend to agree with what they've written throughout the book?

*Why would a merciful God allow Job's family and fortune to be taken away, and why would God ask Abraham to kill his own son?*

## Rebecca Bowman Woods

Want to be blessed? All you have to do is ask. Do all the right things and you'll receive everything you desire—health, wealth, and happiness. Maybe you've heard a message like this on television or bought a book making similar claims. Maybe you've heard it in church, too.

I'm all for positive thinking. But faith is not a means of getting what we want from God, and lack of faith is not the cause of the trials and tragedies that are sometimes part of life. Yet the conventional wisdom, linking faith with blessings, has persisted in one form or another throughout the ages.

The Old Testament book of Job picks up an ancient Near Eastern folktale and expands it into a poetic argument between Job, his friends, and God. It challenges conventional wisdom (see Proverbs) with an unconventional wisdom that has always held a place among God's people.

In the story of the binding of Isaac, the most popular interpretation is that God was testing Abraham's faith and never intended to let him kill his only son. But there are other possible ways of looking at the story. Child sacrifice was practiced by some religions in the ancient world. The story might have functioned to make it clear, from generation to generation, that the God of Abraham does not require human sacrifice.

Stories such as the binding of Isaac and Job's reversal of fortune disturb us, as they should. When we consider these difficult stories, we discover another type of truth—one not grounded in literal facts but in humanity's search for answers to timeless questions.

## David J. Lose

### Who is...
**David J. Lose**

*When I was a kid, my greatest ambition was to be in the Olympics . . . in any sport, and as each Olympics comes and goes, I have to cross off more sports that I'm too old for!*

There are few harder questions than why God allows tragedy to strike God's children. The very presence of suffering, tragedy, and evil in the world seems to call into question the possibility of a good and just God. For this reason, theologians and philosophers have, through the centuries, posited all kinds of explanations. These range from "suffering and evil are the natural consequence of human freedom" and "creation is captive to a titanic struggle between God and the devil" on one end of the spectrum to "evil is punishment for sin" and "suffering provides the training ground for the soul" on the other.

While most such theories—the technical term is theodicy—may have something that commends them, none answers the question and problem of evil satisfactorily.

This helps to explain why these stories are in the Bible. Stories like Abraham and Isaac or Job and his calamities provided the biblical authors with the means by which to pose and struggle with questions about suffering and evil, just as more contemporary stories like *Crime and Punishment* or, more recently, *The Shack* allow us to do the same.

This means that if you take the biblical stories about suffering as objective descriptions of God, you miss their point entirely. Rather, they represent the faithful attempts of the authors to make sense of suffering on their own terms.

While we may not always agree with their diagnosis of the cause of suffering (a test of fidelity for both Abraham and Job), we may find some comfort in their conclusions: God will provide what is necessary (Abraham), and suffering—and the righteous anger against God it may cause—cannot remove one from relationship with God (Job).

## Jim L. Robinson

## Who is...
### Jim L. Robinson

*In retirement, I am enjoying the study of classical guitar.
My fantasy is to sing the lead in* Man of La Mancha.

Both stories are allegories. That statement does not address in any way the question of whether either is historical fact; rather, it addresses the way each story is applied within the text. This is pivotal to our understanding.

Also, these stories represent an Eastern worldview and the imposition of Western logic distorts their meaning. Western logic suggests that God is unjust in allowing Job to suffer. The logical conclusion is that we would have done it better—that our sense of justice is superior to God's! I'm uncomfortable with that, but even my discomfort is an unfair imposition on the text. The Eastern mindset would have no problem with the idea of God rolling the dice with Satan and winning the bet. That's just the setup.

As allegory, the story of Job does not try to locate responsibility for Job's suffering. Indeed, if there is a reward or punishment focus at all in the story of Job, it is that God rewards, not good behavior, but faithfulness. And Job's faithfulness is more a matter of his trusting in God's faithfulness than in complying with any set of rules.

In a similar way, the story of Abraham and Isaac does not address the issue of whether a just God would ask Abraham to sacrifice his own son. Its message, instead, is that God will provide. One might build the case that this story marks the beginning of human awareness that God does not want human sacrifice; but even if that were the case, the bottom line is that God provides even that which God requires from us humans—like a parent giving a child money so the child can buy the parent a birthday gift.

### Scriptural References

Genesis 22, 32; Job; Proverbs

### Suggested Additional Source for Reading

- Hubert Locke, *Searching for God in Godforsaken Times and Places: Reflections on the Holocaust, Racism, and Death* (Eerdmans, 2003).

111

## Suggested Questions for Further Discussion/Thought

1. How do you wrestle with the question of suffering? How has the Bible been helpful (or unhelpful)?
2. This East/West distinction can become quite discouraging when first encountered. Do the previous comments help, or do they add to the confusion?
3. If you were given the opportunity to edit the Bible, would you take out the beginning of the book of Job, where God and Satan wager over whether or not Job is righteous?
4. If there can be more than one "right" way to interpret a story in the Bible, such as the Binding of Isaac, does that mean all interpretations are equally valid? Is interpretation just a personal matter?
5. When missionaries are sent to foreign countries, they prepare by first learning the language of that country. When we enter the domain of Hebrew wisdom literature, the experience is not altogether different. How can we prepare to enter this unfamiliar world?

# Question

*Is it true that both the gospel of John and the book of Revelation almost weren't canonized (included in the Bible)? Why? Who got to decide which books would be included in the Bible, and what rules did they use to decide?*

## Craig Detweiler

### Who is...
**Craig Detweiler**

*I love sumo wrestling.*

The first Christians were mostly a persecuted people. They were an underground movement, trying not to be noticed by Roman authorities. Consequently, it was difficult to organize both the Christian community and their scriptures. The letters of Paul may have been collected and circulated as a source of encouragement during troubled times. The memoirs of the apostles were set apart as what we now call "the four gospels."

A canon is a form of rule, standards by which the Christian faith is defined. Early church leaders like Origen of Alexandria were committed to organizing and, in a sense, "purifying" Christian thought. Within two hundred years of Jesus' death, Origen had focused upon twenty-seven authoritative books that eventually formed the New Testament.

Once Constantine approved Christianity as an acceptable option for people within the Roman Empire, it became much easier to gather for conferences and decision making. Before competing notions spread too widely, the early church attempted to establish the biblical canon. Key meetings like the African Synod at Hippo in 393 approved the New Testament as it stands today. The Councils of Carthage held in 397 and 419 also affirmed the same list of historical documents.

What was discussed? The "extreme" or at least "unique" style of the gospel of John may have caused many to pause. It simply does not conform to the shape and structure of the gospels of Matthew, Mark, and Luke. Those hoping to harmonize the scriptures may have argued against its inclusion in the canon.

Yet the differences in style and substance of John's gospel actually enhance my appreciation of all four gospels. It offers a different take on Jesus' place in the cosmos and in history. It adds many singular stories and quotations to the life of Christ. It fills in several blanks found in the gospels of Matthew, Mark, and Luke.

## Marcia Ford

### Who is...
**Marcia Ford**

*I don't like to be licked by anything I wouldn't lick in return.*

The gospel of John was universally accepted as the inspired word of God, but there was less agreement over whether 2 John and 3 John should be included in the canon—not because of their content but because the content was somewhat private and, some thought, of limited usefulness. The book of Revelation was another matter. The Western leaders (from Rome and beyond) immediately embraced it, but the Eastern church (the eastern Mediterranean area) dismissed it.

Contrary to popular thinking today, church authorities did not "decide" on the canon and then impose it on local churches. The process was actually more like a grassroots effort. Individual churches used certain books that they considered to be authentic, and by the end of the second century, most churches were using the books that now compose the New Testament. By the end of the fourth century, those books became "canonized" or accepted as the "rule of faith" for Christians.

With regard to the New Testament, it's important to understand that the early church leaders considered their task to be one of discernment; God knew which writings were authentic, and it was their responsibility to follow God's leading. They did not use "rules" as such, but they did apply certain principles, namely, that the book's author was an apostle or in some way connected to an apostle and that the book reflected a view consistent with accepted doctrine and moral values. Also, the book had to be highly regarded and accepted by the larger Christian community.

## José F. Morales Jr.

### Who is...
#### José F. Morales Jr.

*I play a mean game of ping pong.*

To this day, some churches (e g , Syrian Orthodox churches) have not canonized the book of Revelation, or 2 Peter, 2–3 John, and Jude all of which are in the New Testament (NT) used by Protestants, Catholics, and Eastern Orthodox. The Armenian Church wrestled (and some say, still wrestles) with its canon—still debated are Third Corinthians and The Twelve Patriarchs, among others. The Coptic Bible includes the two Epistles of Clement; the Ethiopic Bible, still more. And the Catholic Bible contains several apocryphal books.

Most of us in the United States come from the Western stream of historic Christianity (Protestant and Catholic). Regarding the Old Testament, the Protestants took their cue from the Jews and adopted their collection (though in different order). Most historians note that an NT canon began forming (not without heated debates) throughout the first four centuries of the church. At the Third Council of Carthage (397 C.E.), the church attempted to formalize a canon based on common usage, previous lists, and theological reflection. Some canon-tweaking continued thereafter. The Protestant Bible excludes some books from Carthage's list.

Part of the reason for canonizing was to respond to what the "mainstream" church (i.e., those in power) considered to be wrong doctrine, sadly marginalizing sincere Christians (e.g., the Gnostics) who disagreed with them.

All this is to say that the conversation about "canon" is complex. Here are my suggestions:

First, honor—and read!—the canon you've received, recognizing that your spiritual parents were sincerely trying to care for you.

Second, respect the canons of other traditions, recognizing that in their unique books they have found life-giving wisdom. As a Protestant, I frequently visit those books. After all, "The source of wisdom is God's word in the highest heaven, and her ways are the eternal commandments" (Sir. 1:5).

## Joshua Toulouse

It isn't exactly true to say that Revelation and the gospel of John nearly weren't included in canonization. Both of these books— along with James; Jude; 1 and 2 Peter; 1, 2, and 3 John; and Hebrews—were more disputed or contested when it came to what should be included in the official Bible for Christianity, but the gospel of John was probably the least contested of any of these. The main issue that anyone had with John was that the troubling sector of Christians known as Gnostics seemed to give it so much importance.

There were many other gospels from gnosticism as well that were strongly opposed by many in the canonical discussion, writings that claimed to be by apostles and claimed there was secret knowledge to be gained. Most Christians, however, didn't believe that there was any special knowledge somehow hidden within Christian writings.

However, despite the uncomfortable fact that this questionable portion of Christianity was fond of the book, there was plenty of evidence that John was from around the late first century, as were the other three accepted gospels, and for most people the four gospels were considered inseparable. And there were plenty of churches using John, as there were using Revelation and the other books that were disputed. Generally, the prevalence and historical precedent of the use of those books in the Christian community is what got them included in the canon.

### Scriptural References

John 20:31; Romans 15:4; 2 Timothy 3:14–17; Sirach 1

### Suggested Additional Sources for Reading

- Karen Armstrong, *The Bible: A Biography* (Grove, 2008).
- F. F. Bruce, *The Canon of Scripture* (IVP Academic, 1988).
- F. F. Bruce, *The New Testament Documents: Are They Reliable?* (InterVarsity Press, 1943).
- Craig A. Evans and Emanuel Tov, eds., *Exploring the Origins of the Bible* (Baker Academic, 2008).
- Everett Ferguson, *Backgrounds of Early Christianity* (Eerdmans, 2003).
- Justo L. González, *The Story of Christianity: Volume 1—The Early Church to the Dawn of the Reformation* (HarperOne, 1985), especially chap. 8, "The Deposit of the Faith."
- Got Questions Ministries: http://www.GotQuestions.org.

- Dale T. Irvin and Scott W. Sunquist, *History of the World Christian Movement: Volume 1—Earliest Christianity to 1453* (Orbis Books, 2001).
- Luke Timothy Johnson, *The Writings of the New Testament: An Interpretation* (Fortress Press, 2002).
- Neil R. Lightfoot, *How We Got the Bible* (Baker Books, 2010).
- Lee Martin McDonald, *The Biblical Canon: Its Origin, Transmission, and Authority* (Hendrickson, 2007).
- Jaroslav Pelikan, *Whose Bible Is It? A Short History of the Scriptures* (Penguin, 2005).
- Pheme Perkins and Marc Z. Brettler, "The Canons of the Bible," in *The New Oxford Annotated Bible, NRSV* (Oxford Univ. Press, 2001).

## Suggested Questions for Further Discussion/Thought

1. What are the books of the Bible you gravitate toward? Why?
2. What do you think of the principles that church leaders used in their process of discernment? Did they leave out any important principles? Did they include any that you would have omitted?
3. Why do you think the authenticity of the book of Revelation was questioned?

*Are Lucifer, the Adversary, Satan, the Beast, and the Antichrist all the same? If so, why use so many names? If not, what are their different roles, and who is in charge?*

## David J. Lose

The writers of scripture used a number of different names to describe the forces pitted against God's loving and good intentions for creation. The differences reflect the culture, time period, and context of the writers and their communities. "Satan," for instance, derived from Arabic and Persian words among the cultures surrounding Israel, means "the adversary," and is used to describe various beings that sometimes tempt, sometimes test, and sometimes torment human beings.

While each of these names may have had specific meaning for the communities for which various books of the Bible were written, in our own time the terms have often been lumped together, and what we "know" about them comes more from extrabiblical sources ranging from Jewish and Christian folklore to Dante's *Inferno* and the more recent Left Behind series.

While there may be some small comfort found in recognizing that there is no single and all-powerful demonic being waiting to jump out at us, we shouldn't kid ourselves: The biblical authors are keenly aware of the strong impulse to sunder our relationship with God, creation, and each other, and the devastating consequences of giving in to that impulse. Little wonder that the Apostle Paul says "the whole creation" groans in anticipation of the redemption and victory over evil that Christ's return represents.

In light of this, Christians can both set themselves against any and all forces that run contrary to God's goodwill for creation—whatever name or guise those forces might take—and faithfully keep on their lips the prayer that closes Revelation: "Come, Lord Jesus!" (Rev. 22:20).

## Jason Boyett

No, they're not the same, though in today's religious culture you'd be forgiven for thinking they were just different names for the primary enemy of God.

The "adversary" is an English translation of *ha-satan*, a Hebrew word describing the biblical entity who seems to act as a prosecutor in God's court (see Zech. 3:1–7). In New Testament writings, however, this adversary evolves into Satan or the devil, God's primary opposition.

"Lucifer" is a name derived from the Latin translation of Isaiah 14:12, a prophecy about a mysterious Babylonian king—the "morning star" (lucerne ferre) who has been cast down to earth. Along with Ezekiel 28, medieval theologians reinterpreted this passage as a reference to Satan, and the name stuck.

In Revelation, "the Beast" is used to describe the falsely messianic world leader who does Satan's bidding in the final battle between God and evil. We know of this leader as "the Antichrist," though that name doesn't actually appear in Revelation.

So in summary, "Lucifer" is a misnomer and probably shouldn't be part of the discussion. "The Beast" and/or "the Antichrist" are names for a man. "The Adversary" (*ha-satan*) in the Old Testament is a member of the heavenly council under God's control, and the New Testament Satan is the archenemy of the Almighty.

If anyone's "in charge," I guess it would be Satan, the New Testament one (sigh).

## Scriptural References

Isaiah 14:12; Zechariah 3:1–7; Matthew 25:41; Revelation 19:20

## Suggested Additional Sources for Reading

- Gerald Massadie, *A History of the Devil* (Kodansha Globe, 1997).
- Elaine Pagels, *The Origin of Satan: How Christians Demonized Jews, Pagans, and Heretics* (Vintage, 1996).
- T. J. Wray and Gregory Mobley, *The Birth of Satan: Tracing the Devil's Biblical Roots* (Palgrave Macmillan, 2005).

## Suggested Questions for Further Discussion/Thought

1. How many of our ideas about the devil, hell, and so on do you think you can actually trace back to the Bible? What are some of the other sources that have influenced our thinking on these matters?
2. While the specific character of Satan may be unclear based on the Bible, it is clear that he is seen as a source of evil. Why is it important, in a monotheistic religion, for someone or something to be responsible for the world's evil?
3. If you believe in an entity or spirit such as Satan in the universe, what sort of agency or power does it have over our world and lives?

# Was Mary Magdalene a prostitute?

## Becky Garrison

Even though Mary had the courage to go inside and proclaim the good news that "I have seen the Lord," (Jn. 20:18), the church couldn't handle the truth that a woman delivered the news that changed the world. So church tradition pegged her as the penitent sinner (read "prostitute"). By some accounts, she's the woman caught in adultery who is about to be stoned before Jesus saved her (Jn. 7:53–8:11) or the sinful woman who anointed Jesus' feet with perfume and her tears (Lk. 7:36–50).

But if this was case, then why is she not identified by name in these instances, yet she's referenced elsewhere in the Bible? Yes, Luke reports that she had seven demons come out of her but he's silent on the nature of her disease (Lk. 8:1–3).

Given that history seems to have been written by the winners, the church tends to focus on the male disciples. As we know, they ran for the hills. All too often, church historians neglect to focus on those women who not only stayed with Christ until the end but also assisted in the burial of the only man who truly embraced them as equals in the kingdom of God. Even the disciples dismissed these firsthand accounts as nonsense, demonstrating the lack of respect accorded to women in first century Judea (Lk. 24:11).

And while we're at it, let's put an end to this gnostic nonsense that she was married to Jesus. Since when did *The Last Temptation of Christ* and *The Da Vinci Code* become part of the biblical canon?

## Marcia Ford

### Who is...
### Marcia Ford

*I am an intensely private person whose life is an open book. Go figure.*

Probably the most accurate answer to that is that we don't know for sure. However, the contemporary consensus is that she was not a prostitute and that her reputation as such resulted from a sixth-century sermon by Pope Gregory the Great, who misinterpreted several Bible passages. Efforts to correct that have intensified in recent decades, both in the Roman Catholic Church, where the error had long been kept alive, and among Protestants, who often didn't know what to make of her.

This is what we know: Mary was from the town of Magdala near the Sea of Galilee. Jesus cast out seven demons from her. She began following him and has the distinction of being mentioned in the Bible more often than some of the twelve disciples.

Here's what is questionable: Some believe Mary Magdalene was the "sinful" woman who washed Jesus' feet with her tears, wiped them with her hair, kissed them, and poured perfume on them (Lk. 7:37–50), but the Bible never identifies the woman by name. Immediately after this passage, Luke mentions Mary Magdalene (Lk. 8:2), but he mentions several other women as well and doesn't make a connection with the earlier passage.

Adding to the confusion have been artistic and popular representations of Mary Magdalene as a prostitute, such as Jean Beraud's 1891 painting, *Mary Magdalene in the House of Simon the Pharisee,* the 1970 rock opera (and subsequent movie) *Jesus Christ Superstar,* and Mel Gibson's 2004 film *The Passion of the Christ.*

## Brandon Gilvin

There is absolutely no evidence that Mary Magdalene—more properly referred to as Mary of Magdala—was a prostitute. It's an old tradition that has been used for sexist ends but has no real biblical basis.

The persistent claim that Mary Magdalene was a prostitute is rooted in a couple of things. There are seven women named Mary in the New Testament. These include the following:

- Jesus' mother Mary
- Mary Magdalene (Mary of Magdala)
- The Mary with a sister named Martha in Luke 10
- Mary, the wife of Clopas, in John 19
- Mary, the mother of James and Joseph, witness of the Resurrection at the ends of Matthew, Mark, and Luke
- Mary, the mother of John Mark, in Acts 12
- The Mary that Paul refers to in Romans 16

Many traditions have amalgamated some of these Marys, especially Mary Magdalene and Mary, the sister of Martha. It is possible that they are the same person, but we have no way of proving that, one way or the other.

At some point, the church began to assume that a woman referred to as "sinful" who anointed Jesus in Luke 7 was Mary Magdalene. Luke's gospel does not identify this woman as Mary Magdalene (though in a similar story in John, Mary, sister of Martha anoints Jesus, but she is not referred to as "sinful"), nor does it describe the woman's sinfulness as sexual in any way. However, if you are at all familiar with this story, you probably imagine Mary

Magdalene, former prostitute, crying and anointing because Jesus has forgiven her.

For that, you can thank Pope Gregory the Great. In 591 C.E., he delivered a sermon in which he combined these many Marys with the woman of Luke 7, and though the text intimates nothing, he contended that she was a prostitute.

Mary was one of many women who were part of the early Jesus movement, perhaps even on par with Peter as an early leader. Mary also may have been a woman of means, as Luke 8 says that the women supported the disciples financially. John also contends that she had an extended conversation with the resurrected Christ.

## Jim L. Robinson

The idea that Mary was a prostitute is an example of a need some people feel to decorate and embellish the scriptures, perhaps to make them more interesting and appealing. The same license is taken in regard to the Samaritan woman who met Jesus at Jacob's well near the village of Sychar (Jn. 4).

Fred Craddock recalls hearing a sermon in which the preacher said of the woman of Sychar, "She was wearing a short skirt, slit up the side. She wore fishnet stockings and her feet were pushed into spike heels. Her sweater was two sizes too small, and she was leaning on a lamp post, smoking a cigarette in a long holder."

Fred says, "I don't know where he got all that; but I was thirteen, and I was interested!"

Interested, but misled. I wonder how many ideas are floating around in the church whose origin is in that kind of embellishment of the scriptures! All the more reason to read and reread the scriptures for yourself!

### Scriptural References

Matthew 27:56, 61; 28:1; Mark 15:40, 47; 16:1, 9; Luke 7:36–50; 8:1–3; 24:10–11; John 7:53—8:11; 20:1–2, 11–18; 19:25

### Suggested Additional Sources for Reading

- Christians for Biblical Equality: http://www.cbeinternational.org.
- Bart D. Ehrman, *Peter, Paul, and Mary Magdalene: The Followers of Jesus in History and Legend* (Oxford Univ. Press, 2008).
- Elisabeth Schüssler Fiorenza, *In Memory of Her* (Crossroad, 1994).
- Margaret George, *Mary, Called Magdalene* (Penguin, 2003).

- Liz Curtis Higgs, *Unveiling Mary Magdalene: Discover the Truth about a Not-So-Bad Girl of the Bible* (WaterBrook, 2004).
- Karen King, *The Gospel of Mary Magdala* (Polebridge, 2003).
- "Scholars seek to correct Christian tradition, fiction of Mary Magdalene": http://www.catholic.org/national/national_story.php?id=19680.
- Amy Welborn, *De-Coding Mary Magdalene: Truth, Legend, and Lies* (Our Sunday Visitor, 2006).

## Suggested Questions for Further Discussion/Thought

1. Why have artists been so fascinated with Mary Magdalene as an ex-prostitute? What does it say about our culture that this mischaracterization—that of the repentant sexual sinner—makes her so fascinating?
2. Can you remember some Bible stories from childhood? Were they embellished by curriculum or feltboard stories in Sunday school or Vacation Bible School?
3. *The Da Vinci Code* and other books, movies, and Web sites have prompted a great deal of interest in Mary Magdalene. How have such theories affected your faith or your perspective on Jesus' humanity?
4. Can you see any parallels between the portrayals of Mary Magdalene in contemporary society, particularly in the church, and the way that female leaders are portrayed?

*Where are all the miracles today? If they were so prevalent in biblical times, why don't any happen today? Or do they, and we just don't notice?*

## Becky Garrison

### Who is...
#### Becky Garrison

*I wrote my first piece when I was nine. That piece was a one-act play that was an anti-Nixon rant.*

A miracle is *not*

- anything connected to World Vision, TBN Ministries, or any other prosperity "pay-to-pray" preacher;
- a sporting victory, entertainment award, or other kudos granted to a dark horse underdog;
- a genie that appears Aladdin-style to grant your every wish while doing spot-on celebrity impersonations;
- a mayonnaise substitute;
- an annual event that happens every year on Thirty-Fourth Street when Santa rides his sleigh in the Macy's Thanksgiving Day Parade;
- the name of the horse that appears at the end of *History of the World: Part I.*

If we could explain what a miracle is, then it wouldn't be miraculous. Even though the twelve apostles witnessed Jesus performing miracles up close and personal, they never seemed to understand that he was going well beyond simply healing people of their infirmities.

Rather, he was bringing forth a new life that would transform the heart of human history. One might not be physically healed or have one's wishes met, but in encountering the living Christ, one's life would never be the same.

## Craig Detweiler

Prayers for miracles are most often invoked in times of sickness. We pray for children battling the flu, parents wrestling with cancer, grandparents encountering Alzheimer's. Sometimes our prayers are answered in a pill, a shot, or surgery. Doctors perform miracles that bring our loved ones back from the brink of death. Sometimes a patient will outlive a diagnosis. They may bounce back unexpectedly in ways that defy medical explanation. A doctor may call the recovery "miraculous." But it may not make the news.

Jesus is known as the great physician. He battled all manner of maladies, getting quite involved in people's diagnosis and prescription for getting well. We see his powerful healing ministry carried on by televangelists. The "show" they put on seems to undercut the mystery and power of miracles.

Perhaps we don't see or hear about more miracles because too many Christians have made us too cynical. When we put God to the test in prayer, it may put undue pressure on everybody.

## David J. Lose

Two things on miracles: First, I have a hunch that miracles are as much about seeing as they are about doing. That is, I wonder if the difference between biblical times and our own is what we count as a miracle. Today, we tend to think about things scientifically, and so we only define something as a miracle if it appears to defy the laws of nature.

In the ancient world, a miracle was anything that revealed the presence and activity of God. This is most apparent in John's gospel, where he doesn't even use the word "miracle" but instead calls the amazing things Jesus does "signs," as they were pointers, or clues, to who and what Jesus was.

Second, I think miracles have a lot to do with expectations. Biblical writers were not bound by a scientific worldview and they expected to see miracles. Moreover, it was common to report and describe miracles with little concern that one's audience would be skeptical. We have a harder time imaging miracles, and so not only do we not look for them, but we would probably be hesitant to report seeing one.

We live today by the maxim "seeing is believing," but the reverse was truer of the biblical world: "Believing is seeing."

Does this mean that what feels like a lack of miracles is our own fault—that we are limited by our expectations? Not necessarily. But it does imply (1) that our worldview shapes how we experience God, perhaps less through miracles and more through an excellent sermon or moving hymn, and (2) that we might be bolder in claiming the miraculous presence of God in the everyday elements of our lives. If we do so, who knows, we might be surprised by what we see.

## Christian Piatt

### Who is...
### Christian Piatt

*My middle name is Damien.*

As one who tends to be hopelessly pragmatic, I've always struggled with the idea of miracles. For one, they defy logic, which in many ways is the very definition of miracles. The closest thing I've seen to many of the miracles described in the Bible is David Blaine, levitating off the ground or performing some mind-blowing card trick.

Another hang-up of mine is the idea that while some receive sight or new life, millions of others continue to suffer without such miracles. Does this mean God plays favorites? Or were these miracles simply to prove that Jesus had a direct line to God? If so, then why did he turn around and instruct his followers not to tell people who he was?

There may have been a time when people miraculously received sight, walked on water, or came back from the dead. Those things may still be happening today, but I've never seen them. What I have seen, however, is people being healed by the compassion of others, new life springing forth from a mother's womb, and communities emerging out of nothing for the sake of better knowing God and serving others.

It's for these reasons that we named our church Milagro, which is Spanish for "miracle." For us, God's "small" miracles continue to happen every day. It's up to us to open our eyes, pay attention, and maybe even be a part of the next milagro.

### Scriptural References

Psalm 135:9; John 2:11; 4:48; John 6:2; 20:30; Acts 19:11; Hebrews 2:4

### Suggested Additional Sources for Reading

- C. S. Lewis, *Miracles* (HarperCollins, 2001).
- N. T. Wright, *Surprised by Hope: Rethinking Heaven, the Resurrection, and the Mission of the Church* (HarperOne, 2008).
- Philip Yancey, *Disappointment with God* (Zondervan, 1997).

## Suggested Questions for Further Discussion/Thought

1. What are signs that Jesus is at work transforming the world today?
2. What in your everyday life discloses the presence and purpose of God?
3. Are there any miracle stories in the Bible that have been more formative than others in your understanding of Jesus and God? Explain.
4. Have you ever witnessed a miracle?
5. Does the performance of miracles show God's favoritism? Why or why not?

# Are there any mistakes in the Bible? Like what?

## David J. Lose

That depends upon what you mean. If by "mistake" you mean that biblical authors wrote something they didn't intend, then no. But if you mean that there are things in the Bible that aren't factually accurate, then the answer is yes.

Before getting too upset by this, it's important to keep in mind that factual accuracy, as we understand it today, is a relatively modern invention. Prior to the Enlightenment and the rise of a scientific worldview, people didn't think in terms of facts that could be verified but rather in terms of truth that could be believed.

Nowhere in its pages does the Bible claim to be a science or history textbook. Rather, it is a collection of the confessions of Israel and the early church about what God was up to in the world. Near the end of his gospel, John doesn't say he wrote "in order to prove beyond a shadow of a doubt that Jesus is the messiah." Instead he writes, "so that you may believe . . ." (Jn. 20:30–31).

The question to ask, then, when one encounters an apparent mistake is not, "Is this accurate?" but rather, "What is the author trying to confess about God?"

For instance, Matthew, Mark, and Luke all say that Jesus was crucified on the Passover. John, however, says it was the day before the Passover. Did John make a mistake? No, he was making a confession that Jesus is the Passover lamb who takes away the sin of the world, and so in his account Jesus dies the evening before Passover, at the exact time the Passover lambs were slaughtered. John didn't make a mistake; he made a confession of faith.

## Rebecca Bowman Woods

The biblical text has a long and sometimes controversial history. Original manuscripts were copied and recopied over centuries. According to scholar and author Bart Ehrman, in his book *Misquoting Jesus*, there are more than fifty-seven hundred Greek manuscripts of the New Testament alone. So it's no surprise that errors were introduced. And that's before the texts were translated into Latin, and later, the King's English.

On top of errors introduced in the process of reproducing and translating, some copyists made editorial changes—adding their own interpretations and embellishments, and deleting or changing passages to make the text more socially acceptable.

For example, check out Romans 16:7. Does your Bible read "Greet Andronicus and Junias," or "Greet Andronicus and Junia"? It's not simply a letter being added or subtracted. Junia was a common Latin name for women; Junias is assumed to be a man's name, but there are no instances of this name in ancient literature.[2] Why does it matter? Because Junia is the only female apostle mentioned in the New Testament. Erasing her, and the scriptural argument that women were apostles, was as simple as adding a letter.

All of this can hardly be reassuring to anyone who wants to read and interpret the Bible with confidence and use it as a basis for living. I recommend buying a good study Bible, translated and compiled by a panel of scholars (not just one or two). Study Bibles have footnotes explaining where variations in the text are significant. Of course, this doesn't mean you can't enjoy reading *The Message* or the traditional *King James Version,* or other paraphrases or translations.

# Jason Boyett

Some Christians believe that because the Bible was inspired by God, it cannot contain mistakes or contradictions. Why? Because God is perfect, and something God "wrote" must be perfect. But, inspiration aside, we should remember that scripture was written by men over centuries, during a primitive time. It seems logical that some passages may not agree with each other.

Some mistakes can be explained based on the primitive science of the time—for example, biblical writers thought the sun revolved around the earth. Today we know better. But other mistakes are due to factual inconsistencies from one passage to another. A famous one is the account of the "Cleansing of the Temple."

Matthew, Mark, and Luke report that this event occurred in the week before Jesus was crucified, at the end of his ministry (Mt. 21:12–13). But in John, this event takes place at the beginning of Jesus' ministry (Jn. 2:12–25). The rational explanation is that John got the chronology wrong, or altered the timeline for theological/literary reasons. But biblical literalists, attempting to prove the Bible is without error, explain the contradiction by saying Jesus cleansed the temple twice—once at the beginning of his ministry and then again at the end.

Remember that the gospel accounts were written decades after the time of Christ and passed along largely via storytelling. It seems reasonable that some of the details among different accounts wouldn't match up exactly. Less

---

2. Heidi Bright Parales, *Hidden Voices: Biblical Women and Our Christian Heritage* (Macon, Ga.: Smyth & Helwys, 1998), 65–66.

reasonable are the interpretive gymnastics required to harmonize these contradictions in the name of "perfection."

# Jim L. Robinson

Bottom line: We are not justified on the basis of the accuracy of our biblical interpretations. We are justified by trusting in the grace of God. In my own observation, when this question comes up the one defending the scripture is virtually always really defending himself. (e.g., I believe in grace; but just in case, I want to make sure that I'm 100 percent correct in my understanding of doctrine.) The nagging question of assurance is always taunting; what if you're wrong?

The Bible is not a "fact sheet" about God. It is a witness to human experiences of the presence and action of God. God interacts with people, those people recognize and understand (being inspired) the meaning or purpose of that presence and action, and then they record the experience. In the past, some of those records were collected and became accepted as "scripture"—the Bible. Those kinds of experiences—and the record of the same—continue today.

For the most part, scripture emerged out of Eastern worldviews, whereas we in North America are the products of Greek, or Western, worldviews. The question of "mistakes" imposes a Western worldview onto a basically Eastern document, and is, indeed, irrelevant insofar as it relates to experience. Any perceived contradiction within scripture, or between scripture and experience, is more a measure of our preconceived, often errant, assumptions (based on Western logic) than of the content or intent of scripture.

## Scriptural References

Matthew 28; Mark 16; Luke 24; John 20 (four resurrection accounts); Matthew 26:17–19; Mark 14:12–16; Luke 22:7–13; John 19:31; 20:30–31; Romans 16:7

## Suggested Additional Sources for Reading

- Michael Joseph Brown, *What They Don't Tell You: A Survivor's Guide to Biblical Studies* (Westminster John Knox Press, 2000).
- Bart D. Ehrman, *Jesus, Interrupted: Revealing the Hidden Contradictions in the Bible (and Why We Don't Know about Them)* (HarperOne, 2010).
- Bart D. Ehrman, *Misquoting Jesus: The Story behind Who Changed the Bible and Why* (HarperOne, 2007).
- David J. Lose, *Making Sense of Scripture: Big Questions about the Book of Faith* (Fortress Press, 2009).
- Luther Seminary: http://www.EntertheBible.org.

- *The New Interpreter's Study Bible: New Revised Standard Version with Apocrypha* (Abingdon Press, 2003).
- Heidi Bright Parales, *Hidden Voices: Biblical Women and Our Christian Heritage* (Smyth & Helwys, 1998).

## Suggested Questions for Further Discussion/Thought

1. Is there a difference between "truth" and "fact"? Can parts of the Bible be "true" whether they are "fact" or not?
2. Why do you think it is so important for some Christians to try to prove that the Bible is factually accurate about everything?
3. To what extent is your faith based on the factual accuracy of the Bible as opposed to the message of the Bible?
4. To the extent that faith relies on the scripture, how do we deal with the fact that the Bible we use may not say exactly what was said or written centuries ago?
5. Do you believe that the errors and changes to the Bible can be explained by saying they are part of God's plan? Why or why not?

*In some cases, Paul (the purported author of many New Testament books) seems to support women in leadership roles in church, and in others, he says they have no place. Which is it? And why the seeming contradiction?*

## Becky Garrison

Paul's demonstrated support of Lydia, Phoebe, Prisca (Priscilla), and Chloe illuminates the pivotal role that women played in those early churches formed after Pentecost (see Acts 16:40; Rom. 16:1–16 and 1 Cor. 1:11). His other references to women in ministry need to be assessed against the sociopolitical background of Greco-Roman culture.

A commandment such as the requirement that women should cover their heads (1 Cor. 11:3–16) encourages women to follow societal norms. A woman with an uncovered head would draw undue attention to the followers of a religion that was being persecuted by the Roman Empire. Hence, Paul is addressing a specific congregational concern instead of making global pronouncements that are applicable to the entire body of Christ.

Also, one must look at the authenticity of these letters. Romans, 1 and 2 Corinthians, Galatians, Philippians, 1 Thessalonians, and Philemon are seen as "undisputed," meaning there's a consensus among scholars that they can be attributed to Paul. A letter such as Ephesians, which requires women to submit to their husbands (Eph. 5:22–33), is a letter that some scholars believe was either written or edited at a later date.

As the church became more closely aligned with empire, it began to tone down some of its more radical teachings, such as the full equality of all in Christ.

## David J. Lose

Keep in mind two things when reading Paul. First, he's a missionary, not a systematic theologian. Second, Paul anticipates Jesus' imminent return, so his top priority is sharing the good news with as many people as possible.

Today, we tend to read Paul as though he set out to write a timeless theological treatise when he was, instead, providing pastoral responses to particular and often complicated circumstances. This means that we may read as universal and eternal those ethical and theological instructions that Paul intended as particular and provisional.

As far as we can tell, Paul assumed and welcomed women leaders in ministry. Consider, for instance, the baptismal formula he repeats to the Galatians (and the departure from traditional gender hierarchies of the day it represents): "As many of you as were baptized into Christ have clothed your-selves with Christ. There is no longer Jew or Greek, there is no longer slave or free, there is no longer male and female; for all of you are one in Christ Jesus" (Gal. 3:27–28). Keep in mind, also, that Paul names one of his female compan-ions, Junia, as an apostle (Rom. 16:7).

At the same time, if Paul was concerned that this change in social pat-terns would prove an impediment to the spread of the gospel in a community like Corinth, he would counsel that women keep their heads veiled as a sign of their continued secondary status until full liberation when Christ (soon!) came again (1 Cor. 11:2–16).

After Paul's time, there was a split among early Christians regarding gender equality. The author of the Letter to Timothy (attributed to Paul—in the ancient world, it was not uncommon to write in the name of one's teacher) constrains that equality, a view that eventually became normative in the early church.

## Joshua Toulouse

Throughout Paul's writings, there are many references to women as leaders in the church and as ideal role models for Christians to follow. There are also a couple of verses attributed to Paul that are not at all supportive of women's roles in the church.

The problematic verses are 1 Corinthians 14:34–36 and 1 Timothy 2:12, 15. Most scholars do not believe that 1 and 2 Timothy are actually written by Paul. These verses state that a woman shouldn't be allowed to teach. No one doubts that Paul wrote 1 Corinthians, however, so the verse that states that women should be silent in church and that it is shameful for them to speak is still problematic. It's also very contradictory to the many times when Paul men-tions women leaders in an affirming way.

While it is agreed that the letter to Corinth was written by Paul, it is now believed that this section was a later addition. First, it contradicts an earlier section of the letter (1 Cor. 11:5, 13) that acknowledges that women do pray and prophesy. Also, this section seems to disrupt the sequence in 14:31–33, 37–40; while those are about prophets and prophesy, 34–36 seems completely out of place.

Finally, these sections are not present in all manuscripts of this letter. It is likely that Paul did not write these verses against women, since there are many more instances of scripture in which Paul speaks about women leaders.

## José F. Morales Jr. ·

### Who is...
#### José F. Morales Jr.

*I have two quirks that complement each other:*
*I hate the smell of food on my hands and I love*
*the smell of institutional hand soap.*

First things first: The Bible was written by men reared in a strongly patriarchal society. Therefore, we should read scripture with what feminists call "a hermeneutic of suspicion," weeding out the dangerous patriarchal elements.

With this said, Paul, of all people, was a powerful witness for equality. When Paul declares that there is therefore "no longer male or female" (Gal. 3:26–28), he became the first in antiquity to pronounce equality. Moreover, Paul worked with women and called them "prophets," "deacons," and "apostles." Paul considered Junia "prominent among the apostles" (Rom. 16:7). He also mentioned Priscilla before her husband Aquila (Rom. 16:3), which is significant. Paul affirms female leadership.

Having said this, there are antiwomen texts included in scripture, but so are all those passages that affirm female leadership. So we ultimately make a choice. In *The Good Book*, Peter Gomes separates biblical practice from biblical principle, noting that even though a couple of texts speak to the contrary, the early church overwhelmingly practiced inclusion, making the early Christian gatherings "the most egalitarian groups of their day" (Wills, *What Paul Meant*, 90).

In this case, I think the church should preach what it practices.

## Gary Peluso-Verdend

Let's address the last question first. Contradictions may occur because an author changed his mind over time. Or there may be contradictory stances in one book of the Bible because we are reading two different authors, made less visible to us now by an editor who merged two voices into one biblical book.

When it comes to the role of women in the church, the scholars I follow believe we are reading the latter situation. Some scholars argue that Paul's radical views on the equality of women and men in the church and in Christ led the persons who edited his letters to shave the edges off his radical stance.

In many gospel stories and in what scholars accept as the authentic writings of Paul, women are accorded equality with men. Paul's statement in Galatians 3:28 is foundational: ". . . there is no longer male or female; for all of you are one in Christ Jesus."

Contemporary scholars make strong arguments that this text, and other writings that indicate women in leadership roles—the evangelist/teacher Prisca, the female in a male–female traveling couple in the early church (also Phoebe in Rom. 16:1–2, where she is given the same leadership title as men have)—describe the roles women were accorded. Many scholars take writings such as "Women keep silence in the churches" as pushback forces by later editors rather than as authentic expressions of Jesus' way.

The Bible does not express only one voice. Rather, the Bible is a living book expressing conversations and arguments both within particular communities and over time between communities. It is our privilege to be able to join the conversations and the arguments.

## Scriptural References

Romans 16:1–2, 3–7, 12; 1 Corinthians 11:5, 13; 14:31–40; Galatians 3:28; Philippians 4:2–3; 1 Timothy 2:12, 15

## Suggested Additional Sources for Reading

- Christians for Biblical Equality: http://www.cbeinternational.org.
- Elisabeth Schüssler Fiorenza, *Bread Not Stone: The Challenge of Feminist Biblical Interpretation* (Beacon, 1995).
- Peter J. Gomes, *The Good Book: Reading the Bible with Mind and Heart* (HarperOne, 2002), especially chap. 7, "The Bible and Women: The Conflicts of Inclusion."
- Amy-Jill Levine, with Marianne Blickenstaff, eds., *A Feminist Companion to Paul* (T & T Clark, 2004).
- Alister McGrath, *Heresy: A History of Defending the Truth* (HarperOne, 2009).
- Carol A. Newsom and Sharon H. Ringe, *The Women's Bible Commentary* (Westminster John Knox Press, 1998).
- John Reumann, *Ministries Examined: Laity, Clergy, Women, and Bishops in a Time of Change* (Fortress Press, 1987).
- Krister Stendahl, *The Bible and the Role of Women: A Case Study in Hermeneutics* (Fortress Press, 1973).
- Phyllis Tribble, *Texts of Terror: Literary-Feminist Readings of Biblical Narratives* (Fortress Press, 1984).
- Gary Wills, *What Paul Meant* (Penguin, 2007), especially chap. 5, "Paul and Women."

## Suggested Questions for Further Discussion/Thought

1. Ultimately, does the Bible support or disallow female leadership? How do you make your case for or against it?
2. Would learning that many scholars believe that 1 Timothy and 1 Corinthians 14:34–36 were not written by Paul change the way you see them as "scripture"?
3. What would the apostle Paul say to female leaders in the church today?
4. What do you think Paul's reaction would be to those churches who do not allow women to serve in leadership positions equal to men?

# uestion

*Is God "in control"? If so, does that mean God made (insert horrible thing here) happen to pull off a greater plan? Why doesn't God intervene in a disaster?*

### Gary Peluso-Verdend

## Who is...
### Gary Peluso-Verdend

*When I was young and could handle the calories, I could eat a bag of peanut-butter sandwich cookies that I dipped into Hi-C.*

When I was a sophomore in college, four of my high school class-mates attended a party during Christmas break. There was drinking. I don't remember all the details anymore. But, as I remember the story, they left the party, got into the one car they'd driven to the party, and started home.

The driver fell asleep. Their car moved into cross traffic and was struck twice, and the second vehicle set the car with my classmates in it on fire. It was about 1 a.m. A man in a nearby house was playing cards with his wife when he heard the accident. That man ran outside and saw the burning car. He opened the driver's side door, burning his own hands. He thought the driver was dead. The only other person he could reach was the passenger in the backseat, behind the driver.

At grave risk to his own life, the man pulled the backseat passenger from the car. Very soon after the man and the boy in his arms were clear, the car exploded. The remaining three boys died. The one whom the man pulled out was badly burned but lived.

I attended three funerals that break, and made visits with friends to the boy in the hospital, head swollen from the heat and fingers no longer all intact. I listened to ministers try to explain why God had called these boys "home." I could not buy that theology. In reading I did for class and leisure after that experience, I attended closely to what theologians call "theodicy," which refers to the questions of how to think about God as a just and compassionate God, taking into account the suffering in the world.

Is God in control? For a whole lot of reasons, no. Was God "in control" when those boys died? No. However, was God acting through the man who rescued that one boy? Yes. Otherwise, God screamed in pain with those boys and their loved ones.

## Joshua Einsohn

### Who is...
**Joshua Einsohn**

*I have faced my own mortality and found it to be a lot less spooky than conventional wisdom would indicate.*

When tragedy strikes, many of us need to believe that there was a reason for it. In order to deal with incomprehensible pain, there is a need to think that maybe it's all part of God's plan and that we are just unable to wrap our small, human brains around the Big Picture.

In *When Bad Things Happen to Good People,* Harold Kushner talks about the tapestry theory, which basically says that if you looked at the back of a tapestry, it would seem to be a disorganized mess—many different colors of threads, some of which weave on for a long time and some of which are cut short and knotted off. This is how we see the world because we are too small to see how each small piece fits into a larger work of art.

However, when you turn the tapestry over, it is beautiful and perfect and every thread has come together to make a beautiful work of art. This is how God sees us.

Having lost friends to homicide, suicide, drug overdoses, and so on, I admit that I want to take comfort in that image—that their death only seemed "too soon" to me. But part of me still feels that it's a little mean and condescending. Why not make us capable of understanding the Big Picture so that our pain can be soothed?

So I choose to believe that since we can't know the answers, it is up to us to try to prevent tragedy from happening whenever possible and to give support when suffering happens . . . and hope that someday maybe we will be able to see and understand why.

## Christian Piatt

**Who is...**
**Christian Piatt**

*I met my wife on a blind date.*

I remember how repulsed and angry I felt when I heard preachers claiming that the catastrophic floods in New Orleans were a consequence of the city's immoral living practices. It seemed such a medieval, judgmental way of thinking, and I wanted nothing to do with it.

But on a much smaller, more benign scale, many of us do something similar on a regular basis without knowing it. Ever heard someone say something like "everything happens for a reason"? It seems a comforting sentiment, to imagine God in control, but explain the "reason" to a family who just lost their baby, or to victims of rape or genocide.

In my belief system, some things are simply senseless, meaning that human logic can't untangle them. But that's just it; we get tripped up when we try to apply human reasons to God. In doing that, it seems we're trying to stuff God into a pretty small box.

My favorite stories about God in scripture include those in which God exhibits a restraint of power. God could have stopped Adam and Eve from succumbing to temptation, but instead allowed them to make their own decisions. God could have destroyed everything in the great flood, but instead preserved enough to start afresh.

Not that I take such stories literally, but to me they speak to the idea that although God may not cause suffering, I believe God is in suffering. And where there is God, there always is the opportunity for hope.

## Jarrod McKenna

**Who is...**
**Jarrod McKenna**

*I have the most wonderful wife and son and community that make it possible for me to receive and seek to live God's love.*

During the Holocaust, Dietrich Bonhoeffer said, "Only a suffering God can help us now." While some find it profoundly comforting to picture an all-controlling God (somehow distant from the

**139**

Crucified, the cross being a "necessary evil" done to the Son for a "greater good"), I find that more rancid than the horror of the death of God in Christ.

[Selah]

The lament of Psalm 22, "Eli, Eli, lema sabachthani?" not just in the mouth of a great man, or as a means to an atonement plan, but on the parched lips of a suffering God[!] is a sovereignty too bitter for many to swallow.

Do we really want a God who screams the same gut-wrenching laments as us? Do we really want a God who shares the dark isolation of doubt with us? Do we really want a God who suffers excruciatingly with us? Most will honestly say this is not the salvation we asked for. But this stumbling block is what we get in the crucifixion. This is the horror of the Incarnation—a God whose "control" is the fierce unrelenting love seen in Christ. It is the vulnerable victim choosing to expose the system who is victorious.

The resurrection is the assurance that the love Jesus embodied on the cross, the love that raised Jesus from the grave, will one day be realized throughout all of reality. Until that day, we are invited into the agony of praying with God in the garden that not the will of rebellious creation be done, but God's "kingdom come," God's "will be done" in a world where God does not will every situation, but wills something in every situation.

There is no event in which God is not actively intervening; the question is whether we join in that intervention. The importance of prayer is in creating openings where creation comes into conformity with what is revealed in Christ. "The God of peace will shortly crush Satan under your feet. The grace of our Lord Jesus be with you" (Rom. 16:20).

## Jim L. Robinson

### Who is...
#### Jim L. Robinson

*I'm a hopeless football addict. I attended the first Dallas Cowboys game in the Cotton Bowl in 1960.*

This question emerges out of a mindset that sees our existence as the center of the universe. We can't conceive of the totality of God's universe. What we see and perceive is very limited, but we tend to universalize our own perceptions.

I don't believe God is in control. I believe God created the universe as a reality with which God could relate, not as a reality that God could control and toy around with like a child pulling the strings of a marionette.

Many people are terrorized by the thought of a universe in which God is not in control. But the truth is that if God is in control, I could do a better job!

The universe is the arena of interaction between a God who is totally free and a humanity that God has created totally free. The problem is that if we're free, that means we're responsible. And since we don't always do a good job with responsibility, we tend to rationalize and justify our irresponsibility. It's better if it's out of our hands—if God is in control.

I believe that God has a vision for creation and that when we humans align ourselves with that vision we experience the consequences of living in synch with God. When we try to do it our own way, we experience the consequences of living out of our grossly limited perceptions. Either way, God continues to be with us and to provide revelations of the divine vision.

I've reared three sons and am participating in the rearing of eight grandchildren. All of them, thankfully, have passed through the "terrible twos"—that year of wrestling with autonomy: "I do it myself!" "Me do it! Me do it!" They outgrow that somewhere around their midthirties.

In the evolution of the human race, we're still in our "terrible twos"! God have mercy!

## Scriptural References

Genesis 45:4–5; 50:20; Matthew 27:46; Romans 8:28; 16:20; 1 Corinthians 1:18–30; John 14:7–9; Hebrews 1:3

## Suggested Additional Sources for Reading

- Gregory Boyd, *God of the Possible: A Biblical Introduction to the Open View of God* (Baker Books, 2000).
- Gregory Boyd, *Is God to Blame?* (InterVarsity Press, 2003).
- Lee C. Camp, *Mere Discipleship: Radical Christianity in a Rebellious World* (Brazos, 2008).
- Douglas John Hall, *The Cross in Our Context: Jesus and the Suffering World* (Fortress Press, 2003).
- Harold S. Kushner, *When Bad Things Happen to Good People* (Anchor, 2004).
- Jurgen Moltmann, *The Crucified God* (Fortress Press, 1993).
- Elie Weisel, *Night* (Sparknotes, 2002).
- N. T. Wright, *Evil and the Justice of God* (InterVarsity Press, 2009).
- Slavoj Žižek and John Milbank, *The Monstrosity of Christ* (MIT Press, 2009).

## Suggested Questions for Further Discussion/Thought

1. How would you do it if you were God?
2. Do you want your kids and grandkids to be free moral agents, responsible adults, and productive citizens? Can they do it if they're dependent upon you for anything? At what point will you (did you) cut them loose? How did or might they handle their freedom?
3. For our Muslim friends, the crucifixion of Jesus is horrific, which is one reason they reject it. What role do the crucifixion and resurrection play in your own faith?

*Why do so many religions seem to have such similar fundamental stories, like the flood and creation stories? Are they from a common source?*

## Craig Detweiler

Sacred texts and stories often arise out of problems. Some trials are physical; others are more existential or philosophical in nature. In a world in which weather could rarely be predicted or crops could barely be maintained, an understanding of where creation came from and how it could mastered made sense. The core questions of human existence continue to haunt us all. Death is a great leveler that defies most explanation. Natural disasters add another level of fear and powerlessness.

How do you explain floodwaters that wipe out entire cities? Was God angry? Could any good arise from such devastation? The Epic of Gilgamesh and the biblical story of Noah offer ways to deal with tragedy. The book of Genesis offered a rainbow of hope, an "olive branch" echoed in the animated film *Wall-E*.

Unfortunately, such vexing catastrophes continue to haunt us. A tsunami tested Thailand, Indonesia, and Sri Lanka. Hurricane Katrina tried the faith of New Orleans. A cruel earthquake leveled Haiti. Politicians, poets, and playwrights have all tried to explain what happened and why. We continue to wrestle with such questions of theodicy, how a good God can preside over such random or cruel events.

Even more fundamentally, where did we come from? How do we explain our roots? Religion (and literature) are good at answering the big "why" questions. In the Bible, we have religion and literature combined in powerful ways. We are loved, cared for, and defended—even when it doesn't look or feel like it.

## Joshua Einsohn

### Who is...
**Joshua Einsohn**

*I am a dork. Big one.*

I'm sure that there is a certain amount of history woven into the Bible and that there are some facts included. However, many of the stories are just that: stories and tales handed down by word-of-mouth from the many generations before the Bible was written. The world was a larger and more mysterious place and needed explaining, and the stories that helped best to elucidate the world were the ones that stuck around.

It's like a big game of intergenerational and interregional "telephone." The stories that made the most sense got tweaked a little bit from place to place to fit that culture and that time. The Jews had heard a lot of those stories and adjusted them to fit their belief that the world was governed by one unknowable God and not by many smaller, petulant, human-like gods.

Two thousand years from now, if we haven't blown ourselves to bits, I'm sure they'll have new versions of the same stories to give solace to the people who need to understand why the world is what it is.

### Scriptural References

Genesis 1, 2; 6:5—10:32

### Suggested Additional Source for Reading

- Claus Westermann, *Genesis 1–11: A Continental Commentary* (Fortress Press, 1994).

### Suggested Questions for Further Discussion/Thought

1. Would these stories have different significance for you if they were not literally true? How so?
2. Are there other examples of stories in the Bible that you believe are similar to stories from other cultures you've heard? Like what?
3. Why do you think so many cultures throughout history share stories with "universal truths"?

*Is it true that the word "Satan" is never used in the Bible to refer to an evil spirit? If so, where did the word come from?*

## Jason Boyett

### Who is...
### Jason Boyett

*I believe there is no better food combination on Earth than chocolate chip cookies and milk.*

Honestly, it's not clear. In the Old Testament there is a character called in Hebrew *ha-satan* or "the satan," as if it's a title rather than a personal name. The title is best translated "the accuser" or "the adversary." Mentioned fewer than a dozen times, this satan doesn't come across as an evil spirit, but more as a member of God's heavenly court, subject to God's control.

For instance, the satan needs God's permission to test Job, like a prosecuting attorney under God's authority. The satan shows up as part of God's council in Zechariah 3:1–7 and opposes a high priestly selection. In Psalm 109:6, the psalmist asks God to appoint the satan to find an enemy guilty. It's as if the satan's job is a legal one. He weeds out the unfaithful.

The only place Satan appears as a proper name is in 1 Chronicles 21:1, which describes Satan inciting David to take a census of Israel—an action that God condemns. Oddly, 2 Samuel 24:1 gives a parallel account of this story, but there, God is the one who commands David to take the census.

Like the doctrine of hell, the concept of Satan seems to have evolved sometime after the Babylonian exile, possibly due to the influence of Persian Zoroastrianism. Now known by a proper name, Satan takes on a much larger role as the devil (which comes from the Greek word for "adversary"). From Jesus in the gospels to New Testament writers such as Peter and Paul, the devil does seem to be considered the evil opponent of God, albeit one with limited power and bound by God's control.

## Craig Detweiler

The Hebrew word *ha-satan* is translated as "the adversary" or "the prosecutor." God could send an adversary, like the angel who blocks the path of Balaam in Numbers 22. So how did the concept of an adversary come to be associated exclusively with evil? We see such adversarial behavior in the book of Job, where Satan suggests that Job is not as faithful as he may appear. *Ha-satan* offers a series of tests to Job, putting his faith on trial.

Consider the temptations put forth to humanity by a serpent in Genesis 3. The serpent undercuts the directives of God, asking Eve to reconsider the rules imposed within the Garden of Eden. Such "fast talk" convinces her to bite into arenas that were considered off-limits.

The Bible concludes with references to a dragon, an "old serpent" being locked up in the Revelation of John, chapter 20, verse 2.

Jesus faces an accuser in the gospel of Matthew, chapter 4. This prosecutor unspools a series of temptations—to seize power, to offer easy answers, to rule with a scepter rather than a servant's heart.

Biblical interpreters have traced a line from the Garden of Eden to the consummation of history, with an adversary presiding over all manner of distraction. All these strange and mysterious episodes have been associated with a singular, cunning figure commonly called "Satan." Oblique language refers to "the ruler of this world" in John 12:31 and 14:30, "the prince of the power of the air" in Ephesians 2:2, and "the god of this world" in 2 Corinthians 4:4.

It is easy to equate such subversive activity with a satanic figure. While the biblical writers are content to leave the descriptions poetic and open-ended, artists like John Milton have provided even more fanciful detail and backstory in classics such as *Paradise Lost*. After all the fiery imagery in Dante's Inferno, the satanic figure who rules at the top (or bottom) of hell is encased in frigid surroundings.

## Marcia Ford

### Who is...
**Marcia Ford**

*If I told you the really interesting things, I'd have to kill you.*

Some translations, including the New International Version and the New American Standard Bible, do use the word Satan to refer to the ultimate evil spirit, the one-time angel who fell from grace and tried to assert himself as more powerful than God. The name is derived from the Hebrew word *ha-satan*, which means "adversary" or "enemy" and was expanded to mean "enemy of God."

Other synonyms for Satan used in various Bible translations are evil one, devil (from the Greek *diabolos*), Lucifer, son of the morning, Beelzebub, prince of demons, prince of this world, false accuser, and slanderer.

## Scriptural References

Genesis 3:1–7, 14–15; 2 Samuel 24:1; 1 Chronicles 21:1; Job 1:6–12; 2:1–7; Psalm 109:6; Isaiah 14:12–15; Zechariah 3:1–7; Matthew 4:1; John 8:44; 2 Corinthians 4:4; 11:3; Ephesians 4:27; 6:11–18; Hebrews 2:14; James 4:7; 1 Peter 5:8–9; Revelation 12:9–10; 20:10

## Suggested Additional Sources for Reading

- C. S. Lewis, *The Screwtape Letters* (HarperCollins, 2001).
- Gerald Massadie, *A History of the Devil* (Kodansha Globe, 1997).
- Dennis McCallum, *Satan and His Kingdom: What the Bible Says and How It Matters to You* (Bethany House, 2009).
- Elaine Pagels, *The Origin of Satan: How Christians Demonized Jews, Pagans, and Heretics* (Vintage, 1996).
- Jeffrey Burton Russell, *The Prince of Darkness* (Cornell Univ. Press, 1992).
- T. J. Wray and Gregory Mobley, *The Birth of Satan: Tracing the Devil's Biblical Roots* (Palgrave Macmillan, 2005).

## Suggested Questions for Further Discussion/Thought

1. Images of Satan abound in the church and in popular culture. What image of Satan do you carry around with you?
2. Many Christians act as if Satan is omniscient, omnipresent, and personally attacking them. Yet this idea is completely at odds with the Old Testament account of the satan and with the limited powers and presence of the New Testament Satan. Why is Satan given such influence in today's religious culture?
3. If every human being in the world were locked inside one big room, would evil still exist on the other side of the door? Stated another way, does evil exist independent of human agency?

*Why is it considered immoral to get married or to have sex before age eighteen today, yet in biblical times, people (including Mary) did this all the time?*

## Marcia Ford

The question assumes that it is considered immoral to get married or have sex before the age of eighteen. Many cultures today have much lower age restrictions or no restrictions on the "age of consent," when young people are considered mature enough to decide to have sex, and the "marriageable age," when young people are considered mature enough to be married. In some countries, children as young as twelve may have sex or be married, while in others, the minimum age is twenty. In the United States, individual states determine the age of consent; all fall between sixteen and eighteen.

In ancient and contemporary cultures that place a high priority on childbearing, females may marry or have sex at the lower end of the age scale, when they experience their first menses and can conceive a child. In those cultures, morality isn't the dominant factor; procreation is. In ancient cultures in particular, females had little or no say in decisions to marry or procreate.

While the Bible does not stipulate a specific marriageable age, it does indicate that sexual intimacy should be confined to marriage. That concept, coupled with an effort to spare young girls from a life of prostitution, in part prompted nineteenth-century reformers in the United States to lobby for laws governing the age of consent and of marriageability.

## Craig Detweiler

In our postmodern moment, puberty starts earlier, while marriage arrives later than ever. This has created unprecedented and extended sexual tension. Urges that start in junior high school may not be met through marriage for a decade (or two). It is easy for teenagers to lose heart, to consider such a long waiting game as unreasonable and unfeasible. Biblical notions of abstinence until marriage seem highly unrealistic (maybe even cruel).

Those biblical examples come from an era when puberty and marriage often coincided. Times change, and so do social mores. Our notion of married couples living apart from their parents was quite inconceivable in biblical times. Ancient Eastern cultures were much more tribal. Getting married did not mean moving away or being separated from our roots. It was not the start of mobility. It was more like an extension of a preexisting family.

Perhaps if extended families remained together, young people could more easily afford to get married early. The necessity of a college education also prolongs the gap between puberty and marriage. In the Hmong community, it is not unusual for thirteen-year-olds to get married (and continue living at home). While this may put a strong strain on the parents (and the newlyweds living under their roof), it solves sexual frustration in surprisingly traditional ways.

## Scriptural References

Acts 15:20; 1 Corinthians 5:1; 7:2; 12:21; Galatians 5:19; Ephesians 5:3; Colossians 3:5; 1 Thessalonians 4:3; Hebrews 13:4; Jude 7

## Suggested Additional Sources for Reading

- Age of Consent: http://www.ageofconsent.us.
- Avert: http://www.avert.org (International HIV/AIDS charity; offers great information on the age of consent in different countries).
- Paul K. Jewett, *Man as Male and Female: A Study in Sexual Relationships from a Theological Point of View* (Eerdmans, 1990).

## Suggested Questions for Further Discussion/Thought

1. Recent years have seen an increase in efforts to repeal age-of-consent laws or lower the age of consent in the United States. Some people involved in these efforts cite the Bible's silence on the age of consent as a basis for their beliefs. What do you think some of the results would be if these efforts were successful?
2. What do you think the age of consent should be? Why? How about the "marriageable age"?
3. What are the possible risks that people face in getting married or engaging in sexual intimacy at younger ages? What, if any, risks are there in waiting until later in life?

*Does the Bible call for sexual purity? If so, what qualifies as pure and impure?*

## David J. Lose

### Who is...
**David J. Lose**

*I was born on the darkest day of the year.*

It's helpful to keep in mind two things about biblical regulations regarding sexuality. First, there are vast differences between the nomadic and agrarian cultures from which the Bible came and our own culture. Consider the following few examples:

- Most marriages were arranged, were valued primarily for the sake of procreation, and usually commenced at the onset of puberty.
- Women were considered property, first of their fathers and later of their husbands, and valued chiefly for their childbearing ability.
- Children, also considered property, were essential for the survival of the community, and so anything connected with pregnancy and birth was highly regulated.

Contrast this with some of our own sensibilities regarding choosing one's marital partner, the rights of women and children, and the typical ten- to twenty-year gap between the onset of puberty and marriage, and you soon realize that directly applying biblical norms to our own day and age is dicey at best.

Second, some important things have not changed in the millennia that separate us from the writing of the Bible. In particular, sexuality is a powerful force in human relations. This helps to explain the number of biblical regulations regarding sexual purity and our own persistent concerns about sexuality.

Sometimes biblical norms about sexuality may address our situation. Sometimes the implicit value beneath the regulation is useful but its application is more contextual and must be adapted to our context. And sometimes the value being expressed in a particular regulation itself is bound to a context so unlike our own that we need to seek counsel from another more central portion of the biblical witness.

What remains constant is the confidence that our faith tradition—and the scriptural witness as a whole—addresses all dimensions of our lives.

## Brandon Gilvin

**Who is...**
**Brandon Gilvin**

*I'm a nerd.*

When many contemporary Christians talk about sexual purity, they are talking about one thing and one thing only: sex within the bounds of a heterosexual marriage.

That's why I prefer to think about this in terms of sexual ethics, not sexual purity. Sex has been part of the puzzle for thousands of years, and we keep on asking difficult questions about everything from reproductive rights to gay marriage.

Sexual ethics in the Bible are based on a different sense of purity than we are accustomed to thinking about. The Holiness Code of Leviticus, for example, splits the world into two categories: those things that are holy and those things that defile. There were taboos around crossing boundaries and the boundary of the human body was no different. Bodily fluids, including semen and menstrual flow, could render one ritually impure, though that sense of impurity had little to do with a sense of how moral or ethical a person was.

Another major way of understanding ethics in the ancient world had to do with property rights. Women and children were considered the property of men and men exercised substantial control over their lives. Therefore, in many legal proceedings of the ancient world, including those of the Bible, a violation of a woman (rape, murder, etc.) was a violation of a man's property rights and sense of honor. The virginity of a woman was her male guardian's property.

Men, of course, had plenty of opportunities for sex outside of marriage. Men could take multiple wives, have concubines, or visit prostitutes. However, sex with another man's wife violated that other man's property rights and sense of honor. Adultery—understood only as having sex with a married woman—was a property crime and had nothing to do with a sense of purity.

Ultimately, it is out of another biblical tradition—that of justice—that I think we should derive our sexual ethic. How do we treat our partners? Do we treat them as we wish to be treated? Do our actions show the care for one another's physical and emotional health that we declare? That is at the root of any relationship, romantic or otherwise.

## Christian Piatt

Is there anything in the Christian faith today more loaded than discussions about sexual morality? One reason so much energy is invested in dissecting this issue is because sex is powerful. Not only can it create life; it can also tear lives apart. It can bring people together in a way that nothing else can, and it can also drive a permanent wedge between them.

In addition to the incredible power that sex has, it holds almost an equal amount of shame. On the one hand, we talk about sex being normal and natural, but then when we talk about it at all in a faith context it's usually about all the bad stuff!

People have argued—and will continue to argue—about the bounds of the sexual morality called for in scripture. For me, the one guiding principle is found in Jesus' so-called Greatest Commandment. In it, he calls us all to love one another, to love ourselves, and to love God with all of our being. If we follow those rules for our choices throughout life, chances are that the sexuality we express will be one fitting for a God-created being.

## Jarrod McKenna

Around the turn of the third century, Tertullian said of the early church, "All things in common among us but our wives." Today, the church often just reflects a society that holds nothing in common except former sexual partners. Free-market spiritualities discipline our desires and disciple our hearts with every ad and commercial in free-market sexualities. How we relate to each other and our own bodies is revealed in how we relate to the land. Our cultures are immersed in economic systems whose only relationship to the land is exploitative, disconnected, and focused on short-term profits without any attention to long-term consequences.

Our identities as creatures who are inextricably tied in the web of God's good creation have been replaced by identities as consumers tied into economic empires of exploitation. It is in this context that any talk of "sexual purity" must move beyond legalistic repression or reactionary license for transgression, and must hear Jesus' grace-filled invitation.

In Christ, heaven has begun to flood the earth, and those healing and humanizing waters of God's very presence long to engulf our sexualities regardless of our orientation. Our powerful sexual energies are like electricity. Unfocused, they contain a voltage that can lead to death, but when harnessed can create light (and life!).

The Christian mystic Meister Eckhart wrote, "Place upon your passions the bride of love." Sexual purity is not the equivalent to a libido blackout;

rather, it is the discipline of letting the God who is love channel the electricity of our sexuality into a force of kingdom-seeking compassionate justice to light up our world.

Dietrich Bonhoeffer remarked, "The essence of chastity is not the suppression of lust, but the total orientation of one's life towards a goal." That goal in the life of the disciple is seeking first the kingdom of God. A "kingdom purity" provides an alternative to both repression and transgression and will be marked by humanizing transparency and the transforming power of grace.

## Scriptural References

Leviticus 17—26; Deuteronomy 22; Matthew 5:27–30; 2 Corinthians 10:5

## Suggested Additional Sources for Reading

- Wendell Berry, *Sex, Economy, Freedom, and Community* (Pantheon Books, 1994).
- William Countryman, *Dirt, Greed, and Sex* (Fortress Press, 1988).
- Heather Godsey and Laura Blackwell Pickrel, eds., *Oh God, Oh God, Oh God! Young Adults Speak Out About Sexuality and Christianity* (Chalice Press, 2010).
- Teresa Hornsby and Amy-Jill Levine, *Sex Texts from the Bible* (Skylight, 2007).

## Suggested Questions for Further Discussion/Thought

1. Can you think of healthy models of sexual expression in the Bible? What are they?
2. Do you think that sexual thoughts are as important as acting on them? Why?
3. We live in a culture that tends toward the extremes of prudish Victorianism or gratuitous hedonism. How can Christians advocate for an alternative view of sexuality based on the whole witness of scripture?

# What is the sin of Onan, and why is it bad?

## Jason Boyett

### Who is...
**Jason Boyett**

*I have known my wife since we both were in preschool.*

Onan was the son of Judah. When Onan's brother died, Judah asked him to procreate with his widowed sister-in-law in order to produce an heir for the dead brother (this was to fulfill Levirite law and was an accepted custom back then—see Deut. 25:5–6). But Onan didn't want to do it, so he would interrupt the intercourse and, according to Genesis 38:9, "[spill] his semen on the ground." Genesis says this was wicked in God's sight, and the Lord put Onan to death.

This has long been referenced as a roundabout prohibition of masturbation, which eventually became known as "onanism." But Onan wasn't killed for masturbating, because that's not what he was doing. He was practicing "coitus interruptus." Nor was he killed, as some think, for "wasting" his semen.

Leviticus 15:17 discusses ways to "clean up" semen, so wasting bodily fluids doesn't seem to have been deserving of the death penalty. The sin of Onan was most likely one of disobedience, dishonesty, and selfishness. Onan didn't follow the rules or obey his family's wishes, and God saw fit to destroy him for it.

## Becky Garrison

### Who is...
**Becky Garrison**

*After having been raised by hippie parents, I went all Alex P. Keaton and joined the Young Republicans in my twenties.*

The problem here is that Onan was being a jerk, not that he jerked off. Had he done the right thing by Jewish law and married his dead older brother Er's widow, Tamar, maybe so many Jews and Christians wouldn't be screwed up sexually.

In addition to spilling his seed, according to the book of Genesis, Onan is also featured in dictionaries under the term "onanism," which means masturbation, "coitus interruptus," and self-gratification. For those creationist types who think God records the number of times they spank the monkey, count the number of biblical references against practicing self-love versus commands to love your neighbor and then respond accordingly.

## Christian Piatt

There have been all kinds of myths around self-gratification for as long as folks have been doing it. The warnings go from grave to absurd, including admonitions like "you'll grow hair on your palms" to "you'll go blind," and even "you're committing murder."

What? Seriously? Murder from fiddling with yourself? In the case of the sin of Onan, that's exactly what many folks believe.

In scripture, the story goes that Onan, a son of Judah, hooked up with his sister-in-law, Tamar, when his brother Er died. He was more than willing to get some physical gratification from the new deal, but because he didn't want children by Tamar, he ejaculated on the ground when having sex with her. God apparently didn't care for his "pull-out" move and struck Onan dead.

There's plenty of other drama in the story, including deceit, incest, and more, but the bit about Onan is the enduring tale that keeps teenagers quaking between the sheets.

The reason that "spilling one's seed" was considered such an atrocity is because people believed back then that the man held the entire embryo of a baby in his semen, and that women simply held their already-fertilized seed. Typical male bias for the period, but nonetheless, this led them to think that ejaculating for anything other than making babies was murder.

Some religions still maintain that sexual satisfaction beyond the purposes of procreation is a sin, though we now know that it takes two to make a baby. Some old habits die hard, or maybe never die at all.

### Scriptural References

Genesis 38:1–10; Leviticus 15:17; Deuteronomy 25:5–6

### Suggested Additional Sources for Reading

- Heather Godsey and Laura Blackwell Pickrel, eds., *Oh God, Oh God, Oh God! Young Adults Speak Out About Sexuality and Christianity* (Chalice Press, 2010).
- *Merriam-Webster Dictionary* (see "onanism").

## Suggested Questions for Further Discussion/Thought

1. Is masturbation a sin? Why? What about birth control? What's the difference?
2. What are the differences between healthy sexual expressions and sinful sexual acts?
3. If Jesus really thought masturbation was major sin, don't you think the topic might have come up in the gospels?
4. Are there reasons to prohibit masturbation even if it's not expressly condemned in the Bible?
5. How does the idea that "God smote Onan because he wouldn't procreate with his sister-in-law" fit within today's standards of sexual morality?

# uestion

## Are some sins worse or better than others?

### Nadia Bolz-Weber

## Who is...
### Nadia Bolz-Weber

*I once flirted with JFK Jr. without realizing who he was. Then I was horrified.*

---

It's important to recognize the difference between "big-S Sin" and "little-s sins." Big-S sin is the human state of being "turned in on self" without a thought of God or neighbor. Big-S sin is putting ourselves on God's throne and not allowing God to be God for us. The fancy Latin that Martin Luther used was *se encurvatus en se*: the self turned in on the self. This phrase describes that state of big-S sin in which every human being on the planet lives.

Little-s sins are the result of big-S sin. However, even if someone managed to pull off not committing little-s sin, he or she would still be plagued with big-S Sin. Yet part of Christianity tries to come off as a way to avoid little-s sin so that you are progressively sanctified until—poof—you are without big-S sin.

For the record, Lutherans like myself do not think this is actually possible, even though it sounds really nice.

Now, back to the question. Are some little-s sins worse than others? Yes. Are some little-s sins better than others? No. (Leave it to a Lutheran to make something a paradox.) But here's the thing: The sin of murder is more harmful than the sin of, say, stealing a saltshaker from Denny's. But the big-S Sin of the sinner who stole the saltshaker is no less than the big-S Sin of the sinner who killed another sinner.

Being Christian does not mean that we follow a really great Sin Management Program. It means that we confess that the grace of God is sufficient.

> [I]f grace is true, you must bear a true and not a fictitious sin. God does not save people who are only fictitious sinners. Be a sinner and sin boldly, but believe and rejoice in Christ even more boldly. For he is victorious over sin, death, and the world.[3] —Martin Luther

---

3. Letters I, *Luther's Works*, American ed. (Fortress, 1963), 48:281–82.

## Gary Peluso-Verdend

### Who is...
### Gary Peluso-Verdend

*I once won a jellybean-in-a-jar counting contest.*

---

Yes, but first let's define sin. In the United States, we tend to think of "sin" and "sex" together. That pairing is most unfortunate, for both a healthy understanding of sex as well as a healthy understanding of sin. This limitation of "sin" to "sex" and, secondarily, to some vices (e.g., gambling, drinking, or smoking) leads us Christians to overattend to sexual sin and underattend to other areas of sin. For example, in a recent national election, most Americans polled did not understand war as a moral issue.

Sin is a condition of broken relationship, the act of breaking a relationship, living in broken relationships, and acting in ways that would perpetuate a broken relationship. By this definition, murder is sin, insulting a colleague is sin, and passing laws that perpetuate injustice is sin. I've heard some interpreters quote Paul to the effect that, since "all have sinned and fallen short of the glory of God," all sin is equal. Paul's statement might be correctly used to argue that all human beings are sinners, but not that all sins are equally weighty. Catholic moral theology has long argued that some sins were more (mortal) or less (venial) severe.

Certainly, murder is a worse sin than stealing a piece of candy. Abusing a child is a worse sin than flipping off the driver who cut you off in traffic.

Consider this principle: The more people are affected, the more permanent are the negative consequences, the deeper and broader and more irreparable the broken relationships, the worse the sin.

## Joshua Einsohn

Well, some sins are a lot more fun than others! (Rim shot, please!) I'm not really one to worry about the afterlife. If there is one, I think everyone pretty much has it wrong. A favorable judgment isn't going to come from specifically taking, say, Jesus into your heart. Taking love into your heart, sure. But all the exclusionary rules that fall under the category of "sin" are far too inconsistent to be what actually happens.

I have to believe that the sin of stealing your stapler from work isn't going to compete with the sin of hypocrisy. I have to believe that the people who claim to do God's work by making miserable the lives of those who are different from them aren't really allowed a free pass when it comes to cleansing their conscience.

Even within the Ten Commandments, some are quite obviously good guidelines but some are a little hazy. Don't kill anyone. Don't take what's not yours. Don't lie. Stop checkin' out your neighbor's firm butt because you might try to do something about it.

Solid advice. Telling your buddy that the hideous item of clothing that he's fallen in love with looks good on him . . . well, yes that may be bearing false witness, but it comes from a good place, so that's gotta be OK, right?

The whole "sin" thing seems to be on a sliding scale to me, but I've always operated under the idea that all sins are not created equally and that the best we can do is to avoid the big ones and try to learn not to commit the smaller ones . . . often.

## Scriptural References

Exodus 20; 21:23–25; Matthew 23:23–24; Romans 3:9–18; 6:1–13

## Suggested Additional Sources for Reading

- Sallie McFague, *Models of God* (Fortress Press, 1987).
- Reinhold Niebuhr, *Moral Man and Immoral Society* (Charles Scribner's Sons, 1932).
- Steven Paulson, *Luther for Armchair Theologians* (Westminster John Knox Press, 2004).
- Paul Tillich, *Shaking the Foundations* (Charles Scribner's Sons, 1940).

## Suggested Questions for Further Discussion/Thought

1. What is the punishment for a sin? Does punishment vary by sin?
2. Can you truly cleanse yourself of a sin? If so, how? (i.e., confession, Hail Mary, asking forgiveness on Yom Kippur, etc.)
3. What is the difference between being in a state of Sin and committing sin?
4. Do you believe in original sin (the idea that all humans live in sin because Adam and Eve were sinful)? Why or why not?

*Who gets to decide which laws in the Bible are irrefutable, which laws are out of date, and which laws should be applied only in certain situations?*

## Becky Garrison

If we truly followed all the laws in the Bible, we'd be turning the other cheek while gouging out our enemies' eyes. So that Christians don't get all theologically topsy-turvy here, Jesus gave Christians this simple guideline for figuring out how to put biblical laws into their proper perspective. "'Love the Lord your God with all your heart and with all your soul and with all your mind.' This is the first and greatest commandment. And the second is like it: 'Love your neighbor as yourself.' All the Law and the Prophets hang on these two commandments." 'Nuff said.

## Joshua Einsohn

To be honest, I don't have an answer to this question even though it's the one that riles me up most. From Muslim extremists who encourage their people to blow themselves up in order to kill "heathens" to evangelicals who preach "Love thy neighbor as thyself . . . unless they're a dirty homosexual," there is so much abuse of religious power across a broad spectrum of religions that it's hard to fathom. Those who claim to be doing God's work have killed millions of people.

I recently heard a powerful Christian leader say that there are three kinds of religious laws . . . the obvious and irrefutable (Thou shalt not kill), the laws that are out of date ("Yeah, go ahead and have some bacon . . . it's cool now") and the laws that need to be enforced from time to time.

When the interviewer asked who gets to decide which laws are which, he said, "Oh, I do!" This is the same man who declared that homosexuals were too immature to understand monogamy. As a gay man, I took plenty of umbrage at the statement and was frankly scared. He pretty much demonstrated that anyone with a chip on his or her shoulder about anything is free to say, "Oh, I do!" and can then use religious law as a tool to perpetuate discrimination and persecution.

In order for any organization (religious or otherwise) to work, you need leaders. I get it. But how do we protect everyone from the zealots who use religion as a weapon while supporting the wonderful people who use it as a tool for love and peace? I know it's pretty lame of me to answer a question with a question, but it's all I've got. And if someone has an answer, the Nobel Peace Prize is sooooo theirs.

## Nadia Bolz-Weber

### Who is...
#### Nadia Bolz-Weber

*I have nerve damage in my face. If you touch part of my left cheek, it tickles the inside of my eyelid.*

Actually, these two guys from Cleveland and I are in charge. But one of them is retiring soon so we have an opening if anyone is interested.

Seriously, there is the Law and there are rules written in the Bible. The Law is anything the convicts the conscience. Lutherans believe that God's Law is written in our hearts and illuminated by God's Word. But there are two uses of the Law. The first is simply to curb sin and, I would add, to protect my neighbor from me. Don't kill, don't commit adultery, don't steal, and so on. The second use of the Law is to convict our consciences so that we know with certainty that we are unable to fulfill God's Law by our own efforts.

Remember that whole "let he who is without sin cast the first stone" thing? That would be the Law. The Law shows us that we are sinners in need of God's grace. It drives us to the foot of the cross where we hear that because of the work of Christ, we are forgiven.

We love to take the law into our own hands. I'm forever trying to wrestle my salvation out of God's hands and into my own by attempting to just get everything right—to just follow all the rules. To do this is to effectively leave Jesus idling in his van on the corner as though to say to him, "If we know what to do to be saved, we'll just do that rather than rely on you."

There are only two options when we think the Bible is a rulebook to follow so we can make sure that we are saved: pride or despair.

## Rebecca Bowman Woods

### Who is...
#### Rebecca Bowman Woods

*My favorite book of the Old Testament is the Song of Songs; in the New Testament, I like the gospel of Mark.*

Over time, religious communities have developed authority structures within which individual leaders or groups decide these kinds of questions. Within the Roman Catholic Church, the pope has the highest authority. But there's also an office, the Congregation for the Doctrine of the Faith, that considers theological issues and makes decisions. Pope Benedict XVI, then known as Cardinal Joseph Ratzinger, headed this office before he became pope.

In other cases, authority emerges from within a religious community. For example, many nondenominational Christian churches decide whom to ordain as clergy, if they ordain them at all. They come up with their own ways of making decisions about what they believe and how members are supposed to behave with regard to the Bible and its laws.

Separate from a religious community's formal structure is its philosophy on authority. For example, groups with a single leader and not much structure may still be very authoritarian, while groups with a large hierarchy may expect members to decide how to apply the Bible's laws themselves, based on their own interpretation, experiences, and relationship with God.

The problem with human authority is that it is prone to corruption and error. Religious systems should always have a legitimate means of questioning authority. Even God is open to being challenged. In Genesis 18:25, Abraham says to God: "Far be it from you to do such a thing, to slay the righteous with the wicked," and God agrees to spare Sodom and Gomorrah if ten righteous men can be found.

Following the Bible literally is impossible. It helps to be familiar with what the Bible says (and does not say) so that you can make your own decisions.

## Scriptural References

Genesis 18:16–33; Matthew 22:37–40; Mark 12:28–31; John 8:7; Romans 2:14–15

## Suggested Additional Sources for Reading

- A. J. Jacobs, *The Year of Living Biblically: One Man's Humble Quest to Follow the Bible as Literally as Possible* (Simon & Schuster, 2008).
- C. S. Lewis, *The Four Loves* (Harcourt Brace, 1960).
- Henri Nouwen, *Life of the Beloved: Spiritual Living in a Secular World* (Crossroad, 2002).

## Suggested Questions for Further Discussion/Thought

1. Is it possible to obey all the rules of the Bible? Why or why not?
2. How do we know we are living a love-filled life?
3. In your own experience with religious communities, what kind of authority is there to decide how the Bible should be interpreted and applied to people's lives?
4. Can it be healthy to have different opinions in the church about how to live according to the Bible? What are some of the challenges of this?
5. What examples can you think of, in recent years, where unchallenged religious authority had negative consequences?
6. What are some advantages of vesting authority in individuals or groups?

## Were there gay couples in the Bible? What about Jonathan and David?

## Brandon Gilvin

### Who is...
**Brandon Gilvin**

*I believe a day without breaking a sweat is a day wasted.*

People had sex in the Ancient Near East, the geographic region in which the Bible was written. Lots of it. And all different kinds. The fact that Leviticus 18:22 bans men from having sex with other men tells us that it was happening.

Particularly for the writers of Leviticus, Israel was to maintain a distinct identity, and this distinct identity was to manifest itself in ethical and ritual practices that created a sense of order: separating that which was good/clean/holy from that which was dirty/defiling/profane. This sense of order was pervasive. Certain types of clothing could not be worn together, certain types of food could not be mixed, and, well, certain body parts were not permitted to comingle.

People in the Ancient Near East also did not have a contemporary understanding of how conception works. They understood a woman's uterus as a fertile field where a man's semen could be planted like a seed. Therefore, the use of semen in another act (e.g., masturbation or sex with another man) was considered wasteful.

As for Jonathan and David, it's debatable. For contemporary readers, this story of kinship in the midst of warfare expresses an intimacy we are used to encountering in romance novels, and for scholars, is reminiscent of homoerotic relationships in other ancient texts such as the Epic of Gilgamesh and the Iliad. Of course, we have to remind ourselves that we also read from our own particular twenty-first-century point of view. It's easy for us to see things in our own culture and then superimpose them on an ancient text.

How ancient texts are read by contemporary readers changes. They undoubtedly speak to us in our situations, but we must be very cautious not to assume too much. The ancient world is not ours.

It's not like there's a sex tape or scandalous text message that will ever tie Jonathan and David together. It's difficult enough to find empirical evidence proving that characters like David, Moses, or others mentioned in these ancient texts even existed historically.

These are stories. Our struggle as people of faith is to consider how we use them to point toward historical accuracy and affirmation of God's presence in the lives of all people.

## Joshua Einsohn

I've always struggled with the story of Jonathan and David and whether or not their love is sexual, or if it was just two very loving friends. Oddly enough, it was while I was recently reading the geek bible (*The Lord of the Rings*), following the story of Frodo and Sam and their intense love for each other, that my mind drifted back to Jonathan and David. Were they gay lovers or did they just happen to have an intense brotherly bond?

As a gay man, I want to believe that their story is meant to show that homosexuals are just as worthy in the eyes of God. There is a moment when David sneaks into Saul's camp and chooses not to strike Saul down, and he is assisted by the "heavy sleep sent by the Lord" (1 Sam. 26:12). To me, this is God's way of showing his love for David; had he not approved of David and his love of Jonathan, one of Saul's men could have awakened, alerted the other men, and killed David. Instead, David gets to pass in and out unscathed.

However, the part of the story that describes King Saul's rage at his son Jonathan for his friendship with David was, for me, downright scarring. In his anger, he tells Jonathan that he has "chosen the son of Jesse to your own shame, and to the shame of your mother's nakedness" (1 Sam. 20:30) and then puts a death sentence on David's head. I'm sure this passage is quoted (perhaps unintentionally) to gay youths today with ultimately harmful results.

It's hard to know what to take from all this, but I choose to believe that it shows God's love for David, regardless of his sexuality. And ultimately, David is given the kingdom and Saul is killed, so maybe that should be a cautionary tale for anyone who picks on the gays!

## Craig Detweiler

The five or six references to homosexuality in the Bible definitely indicate that gay relationships are nothing new. It is tough to know if Jonathan and David's friendship can be equated with our contemporary understanding of gay couples or monogamous same sex relationships. There have been plenty of efforts to reread history, with speculation about the sexuality of Alexander the Great, Michelangelo, and Leonardo da Vinci.

Several recent books attempt to reframe Christians' relationship to the gay community, such as Andrew Marin's *Love Is an Orientation*. He goes through the "big five" passages often used to condemn homosexuals. Marin notes how selectively we apply the purity codes outlined in Leviticus. It is also tough to pin down the apostle Paul's condemnations in 1 Corinthians 6:9–11. Paul employs two Greek words for homosexuality that are not found in any other ancient literature. How can we assess Paul's understanding when there is nothing else to compare it to?

I am intrigued by the choices of the first cross-cultural missionary in the Bible, Philip. In Acts 8, Philip and the early Jerusalem church are on the run, fleeing from Rome. He heads toward an even more persecuted people in Samaria. En route, Philip encounters an Ethiopian eunuch who longed to become part of the Jewish community. But the eunuch's physical alteration made him ceremonially unclean, unable to enter the holiest part of the Hebrew temple. Philip insists that nothing can separate the eunuch from the love of God through Jesus Christ. Philip baptizes the eunuch. How fascinating that the first non-Jewish Christian believer in the Bible is a sexually ambiguous African man.

## Scriptural References

Leviticus 17—26 (the Holiness Code); 1 Samuel 20:30; 26:12; Acts 8:26–39

## Suggested Additional Sources for Reading

- William Countryman, *Dirt, Greed, and Sex* (Fortress Press, 1988).
- Teresa Hornsby and Amy-Jill Levine, *Sex Texts from the Bible* (Skylight, 2007).
- Andrew P. Marin, *Love Is an Orientation: Elevating the Conversation with the Gay Community* (InterVarsity Press, 2009).
- Jack Barlett Rogers, *Jesus, the Bible, and Homosexuality* (Westminster John Knox Press, 2009).

## Suggested Questions for Further Discussion/Thought

1. What role do ancient texts have on our ethical practices, sexual or not?
2. Does it matter if David and Jonathan were gay?
3. What is the message about judgment here?
4. Why do you think homosexuality is perhaps the most important moral issue in our society for some Christians?

# Question

*If people have to be Christians to go to heaven, what happens to all of the people born before Jesus or who never hear about his ministry?*

## David J. Lose

There are different ways of answering this question. Some who are very strict on such matters would say that people who are born before Jesus or never heard of him are just plain out of luck. Others, drawing on a phrase from the Apostle's Creed—"he descended to the dead"—say that between his crucifixion and resurrection, Jesus actually went to the land of the dead to encounter those born before him to give them a chance to believe. (Some early Christian art powerfully depicts Jesus pulling Adam and Eve out of hell.) Still others would say that everyone will ultimately stand before the judgment seat of God and at that time will have the chance to confess Jesus.

Me? I think that it's pretty hard to know for sure and probably comes down to a matter of trust. That is, my question would be: Do we trust the God who has been so merciful and loving to us to take care of people who were born before Jesus or haven't heard of him? I, for one, do.

So maybe, in the end, it's not the best question for us to ask. I mean, rather than worrying about all the people who never had a chance to hear about Jesus, maybe we should instead just get out there and tell people about him—not so much from some fear of people not getting into heaven but rather from a sense of wanting to share the joy, love, and courage we have in Christ.

## Jarrod McKenna

On that day, all who have died were raised from the dead as all of creation gathered around the glory of his burning throne. As the brilliance of the seraphim and cherubim circled above, humanity was separated into two groups. Some started asking each other, "Did you accept Jesus?" In both groups, you could hear people saying,

I went forward at that rally!
I've never heard of Jesus!
I went to church and played in the band!
I was born centuries before him!
I drove out demons and did deeds of power in his name!
I hope I get to go to heaven!

The Son of Man, frustrated with the talk of "going to heaven," interrupted the "babel" and confusion with a clarifying question that silenced all of creation: "You thought this was about going somewhere else? Did I teach you to pray 'Your kingdom we'll go?' or 'Your kingdom come?' I have come to bring heaven here, not to take you elsewhere. Heaven isn't a 'place' that you go; it's the very presence of God that I bring. And now, those who have responded to God's grace and have not dammed heaven from flooding the earth by accepting me will inherit this kingdom of a transformed creation."

The oceans roared with the outcry and joy from within both groups, as some lamented that they had never heard of Jesus, let alone accepted him, while others were so ecstatic that they prophesied and saved souls in his name.

Then the Son of Man, with a voice like lightening, silenced both groups with this stunning declaration: "You accepted me—as a child starving in Darfur, as a refugee seeking to enter your country, as a disabled black youth on death row, as a homeless vet on the streets, as a drug-addicted prostitute needing a meal, as an inmate needing a visit . . ."

As the list went on, and on, a wave of shock rippled throughout all of creation at the realization that the two groups were not separated by their beliefs about Jesus, or grace, or heaven, but by the response to the grace of Jesus among the most vulnerable and oppressed. The reality of this for one group felt like eternal punishment. And for the other, eternal life.

## Jim L. Robinson

### Who is...
### Jim L. Robinson

*I preached in a bar in Rome in 1981, codirected a tour to Europe and the Holy Land, and held Sunday morning services in the hotel bar.*

Concerning those born before Jesus, the common evangelical response emerges out of the New Testament epistle to the Hebrews. Chapter 11 is frequently called the "faith chapter." In that chapter, there is a roll call of heroes of the faith, and in each case the text says they lived in faith. They trusted that God would act to save God's people.

The New Testament is offered as the account of the fulfillment of that anticipated saving action of God.

In an overly simplistic way, those who lived prior to Christ were saved because they trusted the promise, and those who live after Christ are saved when they trust that Christ was, indeed the fulfillment of God's promise.

People do not "go to heaven" because they are "Christians." They "go to heaven" because they trust some manifestation of God's grace. While I do not experience the presence and grace of God except through my faith in Jesus, there are hints in Jesus' own teachings (e.g., Jn. 10:16 and others) that God is reaching out in other ways, too.

Paul and Barnabas in Lystra preached to people who had never heard of God or Jesus and said to them, "God has not left himself without witness." The idea was that God has made God's presence and grace manifest in every time and in every culture. People who trust God on the basis of any of those manifestations seem to me to be "covered."

## Scriptural References

Matthew 5:9–13; 7:21–23; 25:31–46; Romans 8:38–39; Ephesians 2:8–10

## Suggested Additional Sources for Reading

- Dave Andrews, *Christi-Anarchy* (Lion, 2001).
- Tom Wright, *Surprised by Hope* (Society for Promoting Christian Knowledge, 2005).

## Suggested Questions for Further Discussion/Thought

1. Is the primary focus of the Christian life here and now, or on the afterlife?
2. What makes heaven an important concept to people? What about hell?
3. Why is going to heaven the wrong question if you pray as Jesus commanded in Matthew 5:9–13?
4. Is grace inclusive or exclusive? Is its purpose to weed out the riffraff or to embrace the undeserving?
5. If there are any conditions at all, is it really grace?

*There are many stories recorded throughout scripture in which only one or two people were around. If so, did they write down their own stories? If not, how do we know that what is written is what happened?*

## Marcia Ford

The answer to both questions can be summed up in two words: oral tradition. In Judaism, and by extension, Christianity, this takes two forms—the truth conveyed from God to an individual (such as Moses and the Ten Commandments) and God's truth conveyed from one person to another. In some cases, the person who received the truth from God is the same person who wrote it down; in other cases, the writer received God's truth from someone else.

That may sound suspect, especially to twenty-first-century ears conditioned to have greater confidence in written documentation than in verbal communication. But that wasn't, and isn't, the norm for much of the Jewish community. Verbal communication played a vital role among faithful Jews who believed that oral tradition carried more weight than the written word. The Ten Commandments are an example of written documentation, but how to keep the Ten Commandments would be a matter of oral tradition—and of great importance.

Israelites took great care to pass down information accurately from one generation to the next. Through their leaders, God had made it clear to the Israelites that they were to communicate his message precisely. In the same way, once his words had been recorded in written form, the scribes who copied them made sure their copies were exact representations of the original.

## Christian Piatt

It's hard when news travels around the world almost as immediately as it happens to remember that much of what took place as recorded in scripture happened before very much was written down. Aside from a lack of writing implements and papyrus to write on, few people in the culture knew how to write. So most stories traveled the good old-fashioned way—by word of mouth.

Some of the biblical stories may have been passed along from person to person, family to family, and generation to generation for hundreds of years before ever being written down. Does this mean that stories may have changed a little—or even a lot—before they became a part of scripture? That depends on your understanding of God's role in getting the Bible recorded.

Pragmatically speaking, it's most likely that many details got changed, or that the stories were cultural myths to begin with, not so much based on actual occurrences but on larger messages or truisms the storytellers wished to share.

Renowned preacher and storyteller Fred Craddock speaks often of his exasperation at being approached, after sharing a tale, by someone asking him, "Did that really happen? Was it true?" Craddock's wise response was that there was truth in the story. We Western-minded types tend to confuse fact and truth, but there's a distinct difference. Rather than worrying quite so much about what is factual in the Bible, we're better served to focus on the truth found within the words.

## Scriptural References

Isaiah 40:8; 1 Thessalonians 2:13

## Suggested Additional Sources for Reading

- Aish.com: http://www.aish.com (Jewish educational site discussing oral tradition).
- William J. Bausch, *In the Beginning, There Were Stories: Thoughts about the Oral Tradition of the Bible* (Twenty-Third Publications, 2004).
- Susan Niditch, *Oral World and Written Word: Ancient Israelite Literature* (Westminster John Knox Press, 1996).

## Suggested Questions for Further Discussion/Thought

1. How does knowing about the role of oral tradition affect your confidence in the Bible?
2. Does it matter to you if the stories in the Bible are literal fact? Why or why not?
3. Why do you think Jesus often spoke in parables?
4. Do you agree with the suggestion that truth is more important than fact? Can there be truth without facts?

*Why would an all-knowing God begin the process of creation knowing that it would be corrupted by evil and lead to so much heartache?*

## Joshua Einsohn

My history teacher, Eric Benke, answered this question for me on the first day of ninth grade. Why the question came up has been lost in the haze of memory, but it was one of those rare moments in life when a Big Question is answered and you can almost feel the "click!" as something inside slides into place.

He said (and I paraphrase), "If God just wanted everyone to just say, 'I love you I love you I love you!' he wouldn't have given us free will. He would've made a lot of wind-up dolls that weren't capable of choice. But that's not what he did."

Click!

It's up to us to choose whether to love or hate. It's up to us to choose whether to discriminate or accept. It's up to us to choose whether to look out for each other or look out for ourselves. When we hurt ourselves or someone else, in a way, we hurt everyone.

If there is heartache in the world, it's often because we (in the most profound sense of the word "we") have failed. We are flawed and will continue to make mistakes, but if there's a little bit of God in all of us, if we choose to say "I love you I love you I love you!" to one another, then we're truly on the path away from evil and suffering.

## Rebecca Bowman Woods

One early group of Christians, the Gnostics, developed an elaborate group of deities and within that group, the Creator God, or demiurge, was jealous, violent, and inferior to the Supreme God of Truth. The church eventually declared gnostic beliefs heretical, but it's not tough to imagine why the gnostic Christians had a problem with the Creator.

Look around: Wars, oppression, and the destruction of the environment are the result of God's decision to give us the freedom to make choices. Add natural disasters and accidents to the equation and we're left wondering if it's all some kind of cosmic joke.

One of the ways that God created us in God's image is by giving us the power to create. But we also have the power to destroy. Part of our challenge, individually and collectively, is to learn how to use our creativity for good and not evil, but the two often are not that far apart. Our intentions and our actions are positive, but sometimes we still fall short. Other times, the worst of circumstances brings out the best in us.

We want to trust that God has a plan, but those words are cold comfort when we're in the middle of it all. It helps to remember that the cross isn't just a relic of the past, or a symbol in the present; it's God's signpost pointing to the future. We don't know exactly how it all ends, or when, but we do know this much: Good triumphs over evil, life conquers death, and love wins.

## Scriptural References

Genesis 1:26–27

## Suggested Additional Source for Reading

- Matthew Fox, *Creativity: Where the Divine and the Human Meet* (Jeremy P. Tarcher, 2002).

## Suggested Questions for Further Discussion/Thought

1. Is it possible to believe in God without believing in God as creator? What are the advantages of this idea? What are the problems, if any?
2. What does it mean to be created in the image of God?
3. Does God ever cause natural disasters? Why or why not?
4. How can a God of love allow people to suffer?

*Why would stories about a father murdering his daughter (Judg. 11) or handing his daughters over to a crowd to be raped and killed (Gen. 19) be included in the Bible?*

## Gary Peluso-Verdend

The victors who write history often conceal crimes, immorality, and misdeeds. For the most part, that is not so in the Bible! Biblical stories tend to report warts and all, even for beloved leaders such as King David (see 2 Sam. 11–12). With the possible exception of Jesus (and even there you have his initial treatment of the Syrophoenician woman; see Mk. 7:25–30), one cannot find flawless leaders in the Bible.

Rather, we have many stories of sometimes-honored persons making terrible decisions and acting in horrific, unethical, or cowardly ways. In Judges 11, Jephthah made a stupid vow to God that cost the life of his only daughter. Genesis 19 includes the story of Lot offering up his daughters to a mob rather than surrendering the guests who were under the protection of his house.

So why are such stories included in the Bible? New Testament scholar Doug Adams claims the Bible does not present us with models for morality, but mirrors for identity. We are to look for ourselves in biblical stories and see what and who is reflected back. Such reflections help us deal with the people around us and with ourselves, if we can look deeply enough into our souls. For example, check out Jesus' family tree as Matthew 1:1–16 reports it—enough flawed characters in there for a TV drama.

Bible stories may not always point in a "go thou and do likewise" direction, but are sometimes markers for what not to do.

## Marcia Ford

One thing you can say about the Bible—it never whitewashes the evil that humans are capable of doing to one another. But because so much of the Bible teaches love and offers comfort, it's hard for some people to relate to those passages that depict gruesome and despicable actions.

However, the Bible is much more than a source of feel-good reassurance. It's also a record of the history of Israel and the early church, and that record is populated by very real people who sometimes exemplified the essence of evil.

Why are those stories included? The Jewish and Christian leaders who determined the canon of scripture were careful not to censor its words. They believed that each book they considered to be canonical was the true word of God and should not be tampered with. They insisted on leaving in the good, the bad, and the ugly.

In addition to the accounts of brutality against individuals and the atrocities perpetrated against entire clans, the Bible also records the thoughts of violence and cruelty that men harbored against others, particularly those in what are called the "imprecatory" psalms. Those psalms openly express the psalmist's desire to exact vengeance on his enemies as well as the enemies of God.

Along with the vicious accounts, these psalms provide us with a stark contrast to the teachings of Jesus about loving our enemies—and with the hope that even the most evil people can be transformed by God's power.

## Kathy Escobar

I have absolutely no idea why God includes such bizarre, painful, extremely contradictory stories in the Bible. The Bible is a raw, unedited version of humanity and divinity mixed together. These horrific stories remind us of what we as people are capable of. They offer a constant reminder that real life is ugly, dark, self-absorbed, and dangerous, and that left on our own many of us will do things we had no idea we were actually capable of doing.

At the same time, we cannot dismiss that there are passages in the Old Testament that point toward God actually directing people to do what we'd call fairly horrific things, like wipe out entire villages of people. I don't have a simple way to make sense of those scriptures. They hurt. They confuse me if I focus in on them for too long and forget to turn my attention to the bigger story—God's incredible heart and his passionate pursuit of people.

Regardless of the weird, unexplainable ways that God's stories are recorded in the scriptures, the Holy Spirit is alive and well, working through flawed, messed up, confused people.

I cannot dismiss that those passages are there, nor can I dismiss that amid the rubble and pain and destruction of life this side of heaven, there is also so much beauty and redemption. I have come to believe that the weird, unexplainable paradoxes in the Bible are a reflection of the weird, unexplainable paradoxes in us as people.

We are both good and bad, light and darkness, sinner and saint. And so are some of these stories in the Bible.

## Rebecca Bowman Woods

These are two of the most horrific stories in the Bible, especially for women. I was talking with my friend Amy, who is in the process of being ordained as a Reform Jewish rabbi, about the "Banned Questions" project, and I asked her opinion on this one.

Amy pointed out that many of these painful stories about women are in the context of family, and within families, people often hurt each other. Lot verbally offers his daughters to an angry mob of men outside his home. They ignore Lot's offer and try to break the door down to get to the two angels who are inside. No thanks to Lot, his daughters are spared.

Jephthah vows that if God helps him win a battle, he will sacrifice to God "whoever comes out of the doors of my house to meet me, when I return victorious." He probably expected to see an animal first, not his only child. He keeps his vow, but he allows his daughter to spend two months in the mountains, "bewailing her virginity" with her friends. Without any children, she believes that she will not be remembered.

Maybe that's the point. Stories like these need to be remembered. They stand alongside the stories of women who have been victims of violence down through the ages and even today, challenging us to make the world a better, safer place for women and girls.

Parts of the Bible paint a picture of the world as God intends the world to be. Other parts describe the world as it is. We don't move any closer to the former by removing the latter.

### Scriptural References

Genesis 19:6–8; Judges 11:29–40; Proverbs 10:12; 17:9; 25:21–22; Luke 6:27–35; John 13:34–35; Romans 12:9–10; Galatians 5:6; Philippians 1:9–11; 1 Peter 4:8; 1 John 3:14; 4:7–21

### Suggested Additional Sources for Reading

- Douglas Adams, *The Prostitute in the Family Tree* (Westminster John Knox Press, 1997).
- George Fox, *The Journal of George Fox* (Friends United Press, 2006).
- Phyllis Tribble, *Texts of Terror: Literary-Feminist Readings of Biblical Narratives* (Fortress Press, 1984).

## Suggested Questions for Further Discussion/Thought

1. Imagine if the Bible didn't include all of these hard and disturbing stories. Would it make you like it more or less? Why?
2. How can the violent episodes recorded in the Bible enhance your understanding of human nature? How can they help you come to terms with the darker side of your own nature?
3. Why do you think God would have wanted unsavory passages included in the Bible?
4. Do you believe that the stories in Judges 11 and Genesis 19 reflect God's will?
5. What is the relationship between forgiving and forgetting? Are they the same thing?

*Why are there so many completely different interpretations of the same scripture passages?*

## Jim L. Robinson

The question is easy. It's an expression of a human brokenness that is magnified in a consumer culture ("the customer is always right"). The marketing industry has convinced most of us that we are the center of the universe. Consequently, we tend to read the scriptures (and everything else) through the lens of our own self-interest.

Generally, the different interpretations represent efforts to validate previously held assumptions about the texts. Too often the differences are the result of human intrusion into the text.

The hard part is reconciling the differences and moving from opinion to truth. Increasing the difficulty is an absence of consensus standards for biblical interpretation. Too often, Bible study is an exercise in drawing our chairs in a circle and "each one read a verse and say what it means to me" (a quote from Fred Craddock).

How do we correct the situation? I suggest some initial steps:

1. Restore God to the center of the universe: "Seek first the kingdom . . ." Understand that the best thing we can do for our family, our career, our marriage and everything else we hold dear is to put God first. Put God ahead of our career, and our career will be better than if we make it the top priority in life. The same applies for family, marriage, and so on.
2. Let the Bible speak for itself instead of using it to validate what we already think we believe. Our vision is limited. We "see through a glass dimly" (1 Cor. 13:12).
3. Restore discipline to our faith. One becomes knowledgeable and competent in any field through discipline. Why should we expect faith to be different?
4. Restore a sense of community to our faith. Instead of hiring an "expert" to tell us what the Bible says, learn to trust the collective wisdom of a community of disciplined brothers and sisters.
Hmmm. Sounds like church.

## Craig Detweiler

One of the great mysteries is why an omniscient God would entrust his mission and intentions to such fallible people. Surely, someone interested in getting things right could do much better. Perhaps God intended to leave us plenty of room to roam.

I understand why the divisive nature of Christianity can be off-putting. It is not much fun watching people argue, fight, and even kill in the name of God. While it is good to see what kind of mettle we're made of, when such convictions cross over into personal and physical attacks, we are clearly acting counter to God's intentions.

Jesus engaged in the reinterpretation process. His subversive core principles, known as the Beatitudes, offered a fresh take on preexisting truths and maxims. On countless occasions he starts a story by saying, "You have heard it said . . . but I say to you." Jesus built an ethics upon the law that had already been handed down. He continued the rabbinic tradition of inquiry, challenging his audiences to a new way of thinking/seeing/being.

Perhaps this ongoing battle over the Bible reflects the heart of God. It is good to study the scriptures, to get immersed in timeless truths. Surely, engagement is preferable to indifference. But when the ethics of scripture are lost amid an argument about their meaning, we have all lost perspective. And suddenly, we need a fresh interpreter to remind us who we are, and whose we are.

## Jason Boyett

Short answer: because we're human.

Long answer: because we're human and we are reading ancient texts two thousand years removed from their context.

The Bible was not written in a vacuum, nor was it a preassembled holy book that dropped out of the sky one day. It was written by multiple authors over centuries and is a product of their culture, history, and perspective. Just as a first-century Jew would be confused trying to make sense of a modern newspaper or devotional, it is difficult for us to make sense of ancient writings without familiarity with their context.

But the Bible isn't just a history book, of course, because believers consider it to be divinely inspired. This gives greater weight to its instructions and observations but it doesn't make it any easier to understand. Trying to read ancient texts with a modern mindset is very difficult, which is why different traditions interpret different passages in different ways.

The result of these multiple interpretations of passages is precisely why there is so much division among Christians and Jews—all of whom base their faith on the same texts.

# Nadia Bolz-Weber

There are so many different interpretations of the same scripture passages precisely because there are so many communities interpreting these passages in so many times and cultural contexts. The Bible is a living word that breathes meaning into every community that does the work of digging into it. To calcify a biblical text into one single meaning for all time and place is to suck the life out of it.

For instance, in *Literary Encounters with the Reign of God* by Sharon H. Ringe and Hyun Chul Paul Kim, biblical scholar Mark Allan Powell describes an experiment in which people pair off and read a biblical story together, then they close the Bible and retell it as best they can and note what they added or left out. When Americans were tested using the parable of the prodigal son, almost none of them mentioned that there had been a famine in the land. To them, personal immorality, and not famine, was the only factor causing the trouble of the younger son.

But when Powell replicated this test with a Russian group, almost all the subjects retelling the prodigal son story included that there had been a famine in the land. A national food shortage and the behavior it causes are simply more of a reality in the former Soviet Union than in the States.

Can we possibly conclude that one of these interpretations of scripture is right and one is wrong? Perhaps not, because the biblical text speaks truth into the community and context in which it is being interpreted. It is, indeed, a living Word.

## Scriptural References

Luke 15:11–32; 2 Timothy 2:15; 2 Peter 3:16

## Suggested Additional Sources for Reading

- Walter C. Kaiser Jr. and Moises Silva, *Introduction to Biblical Hermeneutics: The Search for Meaning* (Zondervan, 2007).
- Sharon H. Ringe and Hyun Chul Paul Kim, *Literary Encounters with the Reign of God* (T & T Clark, 2004).

## Suggested Questions for Further Discussion/Thought

1. Some of the most controversial Christian beliefs, such as the role of women in the church, find clear support in the Bible. How do we determine if these simply reflect the culture of the time or if they are more universal?
2. What is the center of the universe for you? How is that working for you?
3. How deep are you willing to go in Bible study? Are you willing to consider sources other than those that support what you already think you believe?
4. Take a story or parable from the Bible. Read it with a friend and take turns retelling it. Note what you added and what you left out, and then ask yourselves why?

# Do women need to follow the commands of 1 Peter and submit to their husbands? Why? What does it mean to submit?

## Kathy Escobar

The first letter of Peter 3:1 says, "Wives, in the same way, accept the authority of your husbands." This follows 1 Peter 2:18, which gives instructions for slaves to submit to their masters. It would be just as easy to use those passages to support slavery today, but most everyone is clear that slavery is wrong.

I believe strongly in mutual submission; one of the most underused passages in this argument is Ephesians 5:21, "Be subject to one another out of reference for Christ." The word for this kind of submission means "to obey, to subject ourselves to, to yield to one's admonition or advice, to submit to one's control." This passage suggests that we do that to each other, not just women to men.

We must remember that when Paul originally wrote these letters, they were one long letter, not divided into sections that men along the way decided to subtitle. Almost every Bible divides Ephesians 5:21 from 5:22, which along with 1 Peter 2:18, is one of the most quoted passages about the issue of hierarchy in relationship. The cultural issues of women in the context of Paul and Peter's letters cannot be dismissed, and we must continually go back to Jesus and the message he fulfilled—freedom for the captives (Lk. 4).

It makes no sense to me that Jesus would come to keep half of the population in captivity, unable to freely proclaim and live out the gospel to the full extent of their giftedness. The gospel came to set people free, not bind them up further. We are all submitted to God, and to each other, and that significant and central piece of our spiritual journey must cross gender boundaries. In Jesus, there is no male or female, Jew or Gentile; we are all free (Gal. 3:28).

Taking one passage of scripture and building an entire unhealthy, imbalanced, oppressive system around it seems very religion-like, but completely contradictory to the kingdom principle of equality and freedom for all.

## Jim L. Robinson

Although there is a paternalistic bias in 1 Peter (as well as in Eph. 5 and Col. 3), the underlying theme in these passages is an ethic of mutual surrender. While the paternalistic bias cannot be ignored, it must be remembered that the culture that produced these texts was totally patriarchal, and in that context a call for mutual surrender was a giant step toward a more equitable way of living.

The word, "submit" means to surrender voluntarily, and 1 Peter sets up the whole discussion in 5:5, replacing models of power and authority (chain of command) with models of humility and leading by example. Therefore, yes, women should submit to their husbands, and husbands should love their wives, "just as Christ loved the church and gave himself up for her" (Eph. 5:25).

## Rebecca Bowman Woods

A few years ago, I did the Walk to Emmaus retreat. I loved the retreat, but at one point the women in my group were talking about books. All had read a book extolling wifely submission as both God's plan and a recipe for happiness. I said I didn't believe God intended half of humanity to submit to the other half rather than to make their own decisions, with God's help, on matters both holy and ordinary.

As I spoke, these women maintained gracious smiles, but I could practically see the thought balloons above their heads: "Oh dear! . . . an Angry Feminist!" Later, one of them offered to pray for me.

The question behind the issue of submission is: How did God intend for men and women to relate? Some Christians point to the second creation story in Genesis as proof that females were created to be "helpers" to males and that the woman's role in the fall makes women inferior.

But Hebrew is a far more ambiguous language than English. At another retreat, I met Heidi Bright Parales, a Southern Baptist scholar who went back to the original Hebrew and found room for other interpretations. Genesis 2–3 can be read as indicating that men and women were created to live in mutuality and harmony, rather than in a dominant/submissive relationship. Part of humanity's fallenness is that we replaced mutuality with something else, and the world is worse for it.

Peter was writing to a particular group of Christians who were under threat of persecution. He advised them to stick to established gender roles to avoid trouble; he commanded husbands to show consideration and honor to their wives—something the Roman Empire would not have required.

### Scriptural References

Genesis 2—3; Galatians 3:28; Ephesians 5:21—6:8; Colossians 3:12–24; 1 Peter 2:24—3:22, 5:1–5

## Suggested Additional Sources for Reading

- Christians for Biblical Equality: http://www.cbeinternational.org.
- Rebecca Groothuis, *Good News for Women: A Biblical Picture of Gender Equality* (Baker Books, 1996).
- Nicholas Kristof and Sheryl WuDunn, *Half the Sky: Turning Oppression into Opportunity for Women Worldwide* (Vintage, 2010).
- Mitzi Minor, *The Power of Mark's Story* (Chalice Press, 2002).
- Mitzi Minor, *The Spirituality of Mark: Responding to God* (Westminster John Knox Press, 1996).
- Mitzi Minor, "The Women of the Gospel of Mark and Contemporary Women's Spirituality," *Spirituality Today*: http://www.spiritualitytoday.org/spir2day/91432minor.html.
- Heidi Bright Parales, *Hidden Voices: Biblical Women and Our Christian Heritage* (Smyth & Helwys, 1998).

## Suggested Questions for Further Discussion/Thought

1. What does "mutual submission" mean to you?
2. Wrestle with the differences between egalitarian and complementary views of marriage. Which resonate with you and why?
3. What are the possible negative consequences for women of reading 1 Peter as a description of God's ideal? Are there possible negative consequences for men? For humanity?
4. Can you think of other examples in the Bible where a passage written to a particular faith community at a specific time is interpreted as applicable to all times and situations?
5. Find an important letter or e-mail you wrote recently or one you received. Now consider the letter from the perspective of someone two thousand years in the future. Which parts of the letter would you want them to live by? Which would you want them to ignore?

# uestion

*What is the thorn in his side that Paul describes?*

## Brandon Gilvin

The short answer to this question is: No one knows.

It's an interesting turn of phrase. Paul describes a "thorn in his flesh." Given that we live in a post-Freudian world, and given the preoccupation that Paul has with the term "flesh" and his use of the term in relation to issues of sex and sexuality, it's easy for us to make the connection between Paul's claim of suffering and something sexual.

A variety of theories abound. Could Paul be talking about a woman he finds attractive? Could it be that Paul's feelings for this woman were strong enough to make him consider settling down and ending his preaching? Was Paul struggling with repressed homosexual desire? Is this some sort of verbal self-flagellation in which he reminds his readers (and himself) that he has no interest in indulging in his desires for other men?

I've personally wondered whether Paul is referring to some sort of genital infection or venereal disease. Given Levitical preoccupations with bodily discharge, and even references to infections in the gospels, it is possible.

Paul could also have had a bad hip.

Regardless of whether Paul's phrase is rooted in actual physical pain, it serves as an interesting parallel to his theology of the cross. For Paul, Jesus' crucifixion didn't simply take on historical significance; it took on cosmic significance, and the suffering of Jesus was an act that signified God's solidarity with and divine empathy for humanity.

Much of Paul's rhetoric ties this suffering with the suffering of the early church under Roman Imperial rule and gives it a redemptive quality. Paul's "thorn," whether truly physical or simply angsty rhetoric, demonstrates that he sees his suffering as part and parcel of his ministry. It is what prevents him from becoming too self-congratulatory and keeps his ego in check.

## Christian Piatt

No one knows for sure what the thorn was in Paul's side. Some speculate he was plagued by addiction or perhaps by some psychological disorder. There are even those who suspect he may have struggled with his sexuality or that he was possessed by a spirit who tried to prevent him from carrying out his ministry.

Clearly, Paul was a tormented character, as indicated in the following Bible verses:

> I do not understand my own actions. For I do not do what I want, but I
> do the very thing I hate. (Rom. 7:15)
> Wretched man that I am! Who will rescue me from this body of death?
> (Rom. 7:24)

Whether it was guilt and regret for past transgressions or an ongoing torment, Paul clearly felt that his physical existence got in the way of his spiritual calling.

One thing about Paul's struggle, whatever it was, is that we can all probably relate at one time or another. Who among us, after all, hasn't found it hard to forgive ourselves for something we've done? Despite God's covenant with humanity that nothing we can do is enough to make us unworthy of grace, we are all too ready to pass judgment on ourselves.

Thank God that God is better at the whole forgiveness thing than we seem to be.

## Scriptural References

Romans 7:13–25; 8:38–39; 2 Corinthians 12:7 10

## Suggested Additional Sources for Reading

- Sandra Hack Polaski, *A Feminist Introduction to Paul* (Chalice Press, 2005).
- John Pollock, *The Apostle: A Life of Paul* (David C. Cook, 1994).

## Suggested Questions for Further Discussion/Thought

1. Would some sort of physical infection—especially one with its origin in a sex act—undermine Paul's integrity? Would you have similar reactions concerning a contemporary religious leader?
2. What do you think the thorn was in Paul's side? Why?
3. Do you have any thorns in your side?
4. Why do we often find it harder to forgive ourselves than to forgive others?

Why are (or were) the Jewish people God's chosen people? Why not someone else? Are Christians now God's chosen people?

## Christian Piatt

A.
One of my favorite bumper stickers reads, "You're special—just like everyone else."

Sometimes we decry the egocentric nature of our current Western culture, but the truth is that the desire to be unique, chosen, or otherwise set apart has been a phenomenon of human behavior for as long as history has been recorded.

The Jewish people are not the only ones who claim this sort of chosen status; most religions have some way that a particular group is deemed to be anointed as the select chosen by God. But with respect to the Christian faith, Jews were the recipients of the Ten Commandments, which became a cornerstone of Judeo-Christian faith, and their stories were chronicled over thousands of years in both the Old and New Testaments.

It's no real surprise that those who wrote these scriptures down also are the ones chosen by God in the stories. The fact that men wrote the texts down probably had a similar effect in placing males at the top of the social pyramid.

There are those today who would contend that Christians now are God's chosen, and are even the only ones who are granted access to heaven. Agree or not, this mindset is consistent with the texts of the Old Testament, but with the New Testament, Jews find themselves on the outside of the circle.

Given stories like the prodigal son and the laborers who all got paid the same wage for different work, however, there's scriptural support for another perspective. Sure, we may grumble that affording all of God's creatures an equal measure of grace simply isn't fair, but it's clear, time and again, that our understanding of justice may not necessarily align with God's grace.

## Brandon Gilvin

A.
To understand "chosenness," it's important to realize that ancient Israelite religion was not monotheistic. The religious culture of the Ancient Near East presumed the existence of many gods. A quick perusal of Genesis and several of the Psalms reveals stories that remain in our canon and point toward a polytheistic cosmology.

According to Genesis, The God YHWH (or Elohim, in some parts of the tradition) strikes a covenant with Abram/Abraham that his descendants will grow into a prosperous nation. Abram's household will swear loyalty to Elohim and Elohim will be faithful to Abram's descendants forever. There are plenty of other gods, but Abraham will only swear loyalty to Elohim, as Elohim has sought him out.

One god—out of many—chose to be in covenantal relationship with one extended household out of many. It's not until the Babylonian exile that Israel began to conceive of YHWH/Elohim as the only god in the entire universe.

Christians conceive of their relationship with God as covenantal (based on a holy promise). Such an understanding does not preclude a single God in relationship with other groups of people. Of course, there are plenty of Christian groups that presume their covenant is the only game in town.

Historically and scripturally, I find as much evidence for the possibility of multiple covenants as they might claim for an exclusive one.

## Scriptural References

Genesis 1:26–27; Psalm 82; Matthew 20:1–16; Luke 15:11–32; Galatians

## Suggested Additional Source for Reading

- Reuven Firestone, *Who Are the Real Chosen People? The Meaning of Chosenness in Judaism, Christianity, and Islam* (Skylight, 2010).

## Suggested Questions for Further Discussion/Thought

1. Does God show favor to some people over others? Why or why not?
2. Have you ever felt specially chosen for something? Explain.
3. If you discovered that God showed the same favor to Muslims, Jews, or agnostics/atheists as we believe God does to Christians, would it affect your own faith? How?

# Contributor List, Biographies, and Suggested Resources

## Contributor: Becky Garrison

Professional title: Religious satirist
Personal Web site: http://www.beckygarrison.com
Bio: My books include *Jesus Died for This?* (Zondervan, 2010), *The New Atheist Crusaders and Their Unholy Grail: The Misguided Quest to Destroy Your Faith* (Thomas Nelson, 2007), *Rising from the Ashes: Rethinking Church* (Seabury, 2007), and *Red and Blue God, Black and Blue Church* (Jossey-Bass, 2006).

### Recommended Books, Web Sites, Blogs, and Other Resources

Thomas Cathcart, and Daniel Klein, *Heidegger and a Hippo Walk Through Those Pearly Gates* (Viking Adult, 2009).
Harvey Cox, *The Future of Faith* (HarperOne, 2009).
High Calling: http://www.thehighcalling.org.
Killing the Buddha: http://www.killingthebuddha.com.
Lone Star Iconoclast: http://lonestaricon.com.
*Nailin' It to the Church* (DVD): http://www.nailinittothechurch.com.
Henri J. M. Nouwen, and Michael Ford, *The Dance of Life: Weaving Sorrows and Blessings into One Joyful Step* (Ave Maria Press, 2006).
Proost Resources: http://www.proost.co.uk.
Religion Dispatches: http://www.religiondispatches.org.
Jeff Sharlet, *The Family* (Harper Perennial, 2009).
Sojourners: http://www.sojo.net.
Jonathan Swift, *The Writings of Jonathan Swift* (W. W. Norton, 1973).
Phyllis Tickle, *The Words of Jesus: A Gospel of the Sayings of Our Lord with Reflections by Phyllis Tickle* (Jossey-Bass, 2009).
N. T. Wright, *Surprised by Hope: Rethinking Heaven, the Resurrection, and the Mission of the Church* (HarperOne, 2008).

### Favorite Quotes

Every day people are straying away from the church and going back to God.

—Lenny Bruce

Always look on the bright side of life.

—Life of Brian

## Five Things to Do to Make the World a Better Place

1. For one day, say thank you to every person who helps you that day, from the bus driver, the supermarket checkout girl, and even the surly person at the DMV. Once you get through that day, try it again the next day. Eventually it will become second nature.
2. Pay it forward by making a small loan to kiva.org. When the recipient pays it back, then pay it forward by making a loan to another person in need.
3. Reduce your dependency on processed commercialized food manufactured by multinational corporations by visiting local greenmarkets, participating in the slow food movement, and other ways to develop a diet that's healthier for both you and the planet.
4. Recalculate your carbon footprint in light of the ongoing economic and environmental crises to see how you can reduce travel (e.g., multitask by making longer trips to one area instead of repeated trips; cut down on conference hopping by using Skype, Webcasting, and other online tools to communicate; explore carpooling and other sustainable modes of travel).
5. Simplify your life—reduce your consumption by seeing what you truly need versus what our consumerist culture has tried to sell to you. Make a conscious effort to purchase items that are fair trade, especially those organizations where you know you're helping a woman achieve self-sufficiency instead of contributing to a sweatshop economy.

## Contributor: Brandon Gilvin

Professional title: Associate Director, Week of Compassion—the Relief, Refugee, and Development Ministry of the CC (DOC); ordained minister

Personal blog: http://www.everydayheresy.wordpress.com

Bio: Writer, minister, diasporic Appalachian, theological progressive, traveler.

### Recommended Books, Web Sites, Blogs, and Other Resources

A. J. Jacobs, *The Year of Living Biblically: One Man's Humble Quest to Follow the Bible as Literally as Possible* (Simon & Schuster, 2008).
Anything by Amy-Jill Levine.
The WTF? (Where's the Faith?) series.

### Favorite Quotes

That is God. A shout in the street.

—James Joyce

I hear leaders quit their lying.
I hear babies quit their crying.
I hear soldiers quit their dying, one and all.
I hear them all.

—Old Crow Medicine Show

### Five Things to Do to Make the World a Better Place

1. Vote.
2. Read a book that takes you out of your comfort zone.
3. Read fiction.
4. Eat local, sustainable food—as often as you can.
5. Find out something about a different culture.

## Contributor: Christian Piatt

Professional title: Author, editor, public speaker

Personal Web site: http://www.christianpiatt.com; personal blog: http://www.christianpiatt.wordpress.com; personal podcast: http://christianpiatt.podbean.com

Bio: I am the author of *Lost: A Search for Meaning* and *MySpace to Sacred Space: God for a New Generation*, which I coauthored with my wife, Amy Piatt. We also coauthored Chalice Press's Lenten Meditation booklet for 2008.

I am a managing editor for *PULP*, an independent alt-monthly publication for southern Colorado, and I'm a series cocreator and coeditor of the new WTF? (Where's the Faith?) book series for Chalice Press, along with Brandon Gilvin. I'm also creator and editor of the Banned Questions series.

I speak, preach, and facilitate workshops nationally on congregational transformation, young adult spirituality, church and technology, faith and culture, and postmodern spirituality. I consult with religious and educational institutions on communications, social media, and public relations. I'm a musician, spoken word artist, and cofounder of Milagro Christian Church in Pueblo, Colorado.

## Recommended Books, Web Sites, Blogs, and Other Resources

Cool People Care: http://www.coolpeoplecare.org (Web site that helps people make simple changes in their lives for a better world).

A. J. Jacobs, *The Year of Living Biblically: One Man's Humble Quest to Follow the Bible as Literally as Possible* (Simon & Schuster, 2008).

Christopher Moore, *Lamb: The Gospel According to Biff, Christ's Childhood Pal* (Harper Paperbacks, 2003).

Taizé Community: http://www.taize.fr/en (Web site dedicated to the monastic community in Taizé, France).

## Favorite Quotes

Be the change you want to see in the world.

—Mahatma Gandhi

If there is a problem and there is something you can do about it, don't worry about it; if there is a problem and there is nothing you can do about it, don't worry about it.

—Buddhist proverb

Truly, I say to you, as you did it to one of the least of these my brothers, you did it to me.

—Matthew 25:40

## Five Things to Do to Make the World a Better Place

1. Listen more; talk less.
2. Care daily for your mind, body, and spirit. An imbalanced schedule leads to an imbalanced life.
3. Give more than you think you can afford, and accept more than you think you deserve.
4. Know where the things you buy come from. One of your most powerful tools is in your wallet.
5. Pray for wisdom, peace, clarity, and courage, but do not hold God accountable for your personal expectations.

## Contributor: Craig Detweiler

Professional title: Associate Professor of Communication, Pepperdine University; Director, Center for Entertainment, Media, and Culture

Personal Web site: http://www.purplestateofmind.com

Bio: Dr. Craig Detweiler is director of the Center for Entertainment, Media, and Culture at Pepperdine University in Malibu. He's a Phi Beta Kappa graduate of Davidson College and earned an M.F.A. from the University of Southern California's acclaimed film school. His comedic documentary *Purple State of Mind* won Best Spiritual Film at the Breckenridge Festival of Film, and the Audience Award at the Tallahassee Film Festival. His latest book, *Into the Dark*, searches for the sacred amid the top-ranked films on the Internet Movie Database. Craig's cultural commentary has appeared on ABC's Nightline, CNN, Fox News, NPR, and in *The New York Times*.

### Recommended Books, Web Sites, Blogs, and Other Resources

Frederick Buechner, *Wishful Thinking* (HarperOne, 1993).
Julie Clawson, *Everyday Justice* (InterVarsity Press, 2009).
Conversant Life: http://www.conversantlife.com.
Anne Lamott, *Traveling Mercies* (Anchor Books, 2000).
Ben Lowe, *Green Revolution* (InterVarsity Press, 2000).
Andrew P. Marin, *Love Is an Orientation: Elevating the Conversation with the Gay Community* (InterVarsity Press, 2009).
N. T. Wright, *Simply Christian: Why Christianity Makes Sense* (HarperOne, 2010).

### Favorite Quote

He not busy being born is busy dying.

—Bob Dylan

### Five Things to Do to Make the World a Better Place

1. Write a song.
2. Visit a prisoner.
3. Become a vegetarian.
4. Join the One campaign.
5. Pay for a child's education (just $30 or $35 per month via WorldVision or Compassion).

## Contributor: David J. Lose

Professional title: Marbury E. Anderson Associate Professor of Biblical Preaching at Luther Seminary, St. Paul, Minn.

Personal Web site and podcast: http://www.WorkingPreacher.org; Sermon Brainwave podcast found on http://www.workingpreacher.org; Bible Roundtable podcast found on http://www.enterthebible.org

Bio: David J. Lose holds the Marbury E. Anderson Chair in Biblical Preaching at Luther Seminary, where he also serves as the Director of the Center for Biblical Preaching. He is the author of *Making Sense of Scripture* (2009), *Confessing Jesus Christ: Preaching in a Postmodern World* (2003), and *Making Sense of the Christian Story* (forthcoming, September 2010). He speaks widely in the United States and abroad on preaching, Christian faith in a postmodern world, and biblical interpretation.

### Recommended Books, Web Sites, Blogs, and Other Resources

Center for Biblical Preaching, Luther Seminary: http://www
.WorkingPreacher.org.
*It's a Wonderful Life (film).*
Leif Enger, *Peace Like a River* (Atlantic Monthly Press, 2002).
Luther Seminary: http://www.EntertheBible.org.
*Schindler's List (film).*
TED Conferences, TED Talks: http://www.TED.com.
The Chieftains, "The Bells of Dublin" (audio CD).

### Favorite Quote

Be the change you want to see in the world.

—Mahatma Gandhi

### Five Things to Do to Make the World a Better Place

1. Pray—for peace, for justice, for equality, for people you know who are hurting or in need, for people you don't know who are hurting or in need, for someone you don't like, for leaders in the world that they may discern what is right and have the courage to do it.
2. Listen—almost every day you will run into someone who needs you to listen—not to agree or disagree, not to correct or make suggestions, but just to listen. Do that.

3. Reach out—almost every day you will come across someone who is discouraged, down, afraid, or sad. When you find that person, say something encouraging, hopeful, or uplifting.
4. Participate—whatever we can accomplish alone, we can accomplish even more together. Sometime in the next week, ask members of a group you're part of—a church group, a political group, a book club, whatever—what they're doing to make a difference in the world, and join them in doing it.
5. Share—find a group or cause that you care about and budget what you can give them each month of your time, your talent, and your money. And then do it.

## Contributor: Gary Peluso-Verdend

Professional title: President, Phillips Theological Seminary; Associate Professor of Practical Theology

Personal e-mail: gary.peluso@ptstulsa.edu

Bio: Gary Peluso-Verdend is the President and Associate Professor of practical theology at Phillips Theological Seminary in Tulsa, Oklahoma. He is an ordained elder in the United Methodist Church. Prior to earning his Ph.D. at the University of Chicago Divinity School, he served several congregations in Illinois.

Dr. Peluso-Verdend is a scholar in the field of practical theology. His 2005 book, *Paying Attention: Focusing Your Congregation on What Matters* (Alban), represents his interests in leadership education, congregational dynamics, social change, and Christian practices.

He and his wife, Cheri, live with their daughter Eliana in Tulsa, Oklahoma, in the third (and last) house-in-need-of-updating they have owned. Gary's other children include Peter, Abigail, and Zachary.

### Recommended Books, Web Sites, Blogs, and Other Resources

Alban Institute: http://www.alban.org.
Marcus J. Borg, *Meeting Jesus Again for the First Time* (HarperOne, 1995).
Robert Kegan, and Lisa Lahey, *Immunity to Change* (Harvard Business School Press, 2009).
Henri Nouwen, *Making All Things New* (HarperOne, 1981).
Phillips Theological Seminary: http://www.ptstulsa.edu.
Salon: http://www.salon.com.
Visions of Giving: http://www.visionsofgiving.org.

## Favorite Quote

A God without wrath brought a people without sin into a kingdom without judgment through the ministrations of Christ without a cross.

—H. Richard Niebuhr, *The Kingdom of God in America*

## Five Things to Do to Make the World a Better Place

1. Take a moment—respond rather than react.
2. Treat yourself and everyone you meet as the Image of God that you are and that they are.
3. Learn to accept forgiveness and to offer forgiveness.
4. In a world drowning in data, learn what is saving knowledge and pay attention there.
5. Practice hospitality as Henri Nouwen defined it: Make a space in your life for others who are not like you without requiring that they become like you.

# Contributor name: Jarrod McKenna

Professional title: Brutha

Personal Web sites: http://www.paceebene.org/user/8; http://www.twitter.com/jarrodmckenna; http://www.facebook.com/jarrod.mckenna; http://www.jesusradicals.com/iconocast

Bio: Jarrod McKenna is a recovering consumer, hack-philosopher, activist trainer, ex-artist, doubting [yet wonder-filled] evangelist, larrikin seditionist, and one day wannabe permaculturalist who is seeking to live God's love. As "National Adviser for Youth, Faith and Activism" for Australia's largest Aid/Development Organization, World Vision Australia, Jarrod works to mobilize a generation to take hold of our vocation to witness to *"God's nonviolent transformation of all things"* by equipping communities to conspiring to end human trafficking, climate change, maternal deaths, and extreme poverty.

He is a cofounder of the Peace Tree Community serving with the marginalized in one of the dodgiest areas in his city, initiated Together for Humanity in Western Australia (a multifaith youth project serving together for the common good), and is the founder and creative director of EPYC! (Empowering Peacemakers in Your Community) for which he received an Australian Peace Award for his work in empowering a generation of "eco-evangelists and peace prophets." Which almost makes him sound respectable . . . almost.

## Recommended Books, Web Sites, Blogs, and Other Resources

### Web Sites

Democracy Now: http://www.democracynow.org
Jesus Radicals: http://www.jesusradicals.com
N. T. Wright Page: http://www.ntwrightpage.com
Sacred Space: http://www.Sacredspace.ie

### Books

So, so many, as well as Holy Scripture, here are my top ten for discipleship:

James Alison, *Knowing Jesus*
Dave Andrews, *Plan Be*
Lee C. Camp, *Mere Discipleship*
Shane Claiborne, *The Irresistible Revolution*
Dorothy Day, *The Long Loneliness*
John Dear, *Mohandas Gandhi: Essential Writings*
John Dear, *A Persistent Peace*
Paul Dekar, *Community of the Transfiguration: The Journey of a New Monastic Community*
Syliva C. Keesmatt and Brian J. Walsh, *Colossians Remixed*
Martin Luther King Jr., *Strength to Love*
Maggie Ross, *Pillars of Flame: Power, Priesthood, and Spiritual Maturity*
Kallistos Ware, *The Orthodox Way*

## Favorite Quotes

For the earth will be filled with the knowledge of the glory of
YHWH, as the waters cover the sea.
—Habakkuk 2:14

If you have come to help me, you are wasting your time; but if you
are here because your liberation is bound up with mine, then let us
work together.
—Lila Watson (Australian Aboriginal activist)

I didn't get my inspiration from Karl Marx; I got it from a man
named Jesus.
—Martin Luther King Jr.

We have learned that the only solution is love and that love comes with community.

—Dorothy Day

You know what the good news is? It's the end of the bad news.
—Ade Leason (Kiwi Ploughshares activist)

The Christian alternative to war is worship.

—Stanley Hauerwas

The future is here. It's just not widely distributed yet.

—William Gibson

The poor tell us who we are. The prophets tell us who we could be. So we hide the poor, and kill the prophets.

—Philip Berrigan

You can't be a Christian, if you're not willing to pick up your cross. And, in the end, be crucified on it. That's the bottom line.

—Cornel West

There is no proof of God, only witnesses.

—Joshua Abraham Heschel

I'd rather go to hell with Jesus than heaven without him.
—OK, no one famous said that, but I say it all the time

## Five Things to Do to Make the World a Better Place

1. Meditate daily on the life, teachings, crucifixion, and resurrection of our Lord. This is something Martin Luther King Jr. had everyone in the civil rights movement commit to, and it's having a powerful effect in my life.
2. Every time you pray, let the Lord's Prayer be a part of it. Let the wonder of "on earth as it is in heaven" infuse this good news into your psyche until it appears in your dreams. And then let God's dream for creation appear in your waking life.
3. Seek to memorize the Sermon on the Mount. I'm not there yet but this discipline of memorizing scriptures I find very helpful and it's an amazing grace when the Holy Spirit brings them to memory while you are working (start with the Beatitudes).
4. Find two or three people who are willing to hold you accountable to acting on a new imagination of grace. Choose small experiments (e.g., become aware of God's presence in those who are excluded at school or

at work and seek to include them) and share them with these two sisters or brothers as you move deeper into the grace of discipleship.

5. Spend time daily in silence, just waiting on the visitation of the presence of God. My experience has been that from this silent surrender, I'm able to be more fully open to the triune God's transformation in my life. It's not easy. I often find it hard. But life takes on colors that slowly replace what was black and white. Both the pain and the beauty that were dull become vibrant and can pass through us in prayer. Our love for God and the wonder of God's grace can start to seep out of our wounds into a love for all of creation, even our enemies. From this silence, let worship well up and over into every part of life.

## Contributor: Jason Boyett

Professional title: Writer

Personal Web sites: http://www.jasonboyett.com; http://www.pocketguidesite.com; jb@jasonboyett.com

Bio: Jason Boyett is the author of several books, including the Pocket Guide Series on Religious History (Jossey-Bass) and *O Me of Little Faith* (Zondervan, 2010). He has been featured on the History Channel and National Geographic Channel and writes for a variety of publications. Jason blogs about faith and culture at jasonboyett.com.

### Favorite Quotes

Don't expect faith to clear things up for you. It is trust, not certainty.
—Flannery O'Connor

I do not feel obliged to believe that the same God who has endowed us with sense, reason, and intellect has intended us to forgo their use.
—Galileo Galilei

### Five Things to Do to Make the World a Better Place

1. Be humble about the Bible. It is a complex book with complex characters and a complex message. People interpret it in very different ways. Feel free to let it speak to your own life with as much confidence as you want. But when sharing your ideas with others, please use humility. After all, you might be wrong.

2. Volunteer outside your church. Do something at your kids' school, or with sports leagues, or within community organizations not connected to your church. This is part of being a good neighbor.
3. Share your life with others, whether they are friends or family or both. They need you as much as you need them.
4. Exercise outdoors. Get off the treadmill or cardio machine and go run on a trail, walk along the sidewalk, or ride your bike outside. I don't know why, but I swear this makes you a better human being.
5. Don't be afraid to do something because it's fun and it makes you happy. Not everything has to have spiritual significance. And anyway, it's often the things that seem the least spiritually significant that end up having the most impact on the world around you.

## Contributor: Jim L. Robinson

Professional title: Ordained minister (retired), transitional minister, grandpa, dedicated bass fisherman

Bio: I grew up in the Southern Baptist Church in the 1950s, where my inquiring mind was a distinct liability. I was particularly frustrated at the lack of ecumenical cooperation, which sometimes went so far as limiting cooperation between other Southern Baptist congregations. My discontent peaked when I married a woman from a mainline denomination (a baptized believer) and my church required that she be "rebaptized."

I finally found my ecclesiastical identity while doing voluntary work for a Navy chaplain (a Disciple) in Vietnam. After military service, I earned a Master of Divinity degree (1972) and a Doctor of Ministry (1976) degree from the Graduate Seminary of Phillips University (now Phillips Graduate Seminary). I served pastoral ministries in Oklahoma and Arkansas until retiring in 2005. I currently work with churches in transition, and spend as much time as possible stalking the elusive largemouth bass (*micropterus salmoides*).

### Recommended Books, Web Sites, Blogs, and Other Resources

Edward H. Hammett, *Reaching People under 40 while Keeping People over 60* (Chalice Press, 2007). Deals competently and constructively with the challenge of reconciling differences across six generations.

Maria Harris, *Proclaim Jubilee* (Westminster John Knox Press, 1996). Harris explores the implications of applying the biblical Jubilee (Leviticus 25) in today's culture—for example, every fifty years the land would lie fallow for one year, all debts be forgiven, captives be freed, and a celebration held.

## Favorite Quotes

Beware the illusion that you can create a system so nearly perfect that nobody has to be good.

> —unknown; sometimes attributed to Mahatma Gandhi

Life is not so much about surviving the storm as it is learning to dance in the rain.

> —Vivian Greene

Life is short; eat dessert first!

> —unknown

## Five Things to Do to Make the World a Better Place

1. Leave your backyard. Realize that no matter how much we want it to be "all about me," life has a distinctively social dimension. Get out "among 'em."
2. Make an effort to become more aware of what's going on in the world—but don't get all your insight from one source. Balance Fox News with MSNBC; spend some time with CNN and each of the network news outlets. Everyone has a right to have an opinion, but opinion doesn't always serve truth.
3. Reach out intentionally to build a relationship with a person from a generation other than yours. Build bridges. Find out why your grandparents like Glenn Miller (my granddaughter discovered she loves "In the Mood") or why your grandkids like "metal" or "rap" without judging or lecturing.
4. Take on a real learning challenge. Take on something written by a biblical scholar or theologian (e.g., Walter Brueggemann or William Willimon). Attend a lecture at a seminary. Stretch your mind from a theological perspective.
5. Join or create a hands-on, service-oriented organization. Go on a mission trip. Get involved.

# Contributor: José F. Morales Jr.

Personal Web site: DJ Rhema: http://www.myspace.com/rhemapresentsjosefrancisco; rhemalogix@yahoo.com; rhemalogix.josefrancisco@gmail.com

Bio: José is currently the Associate Pastor of Iglesia del Pueblo Christian Church (Disciples of Christ) in Hammond, Indiana (Chicago's neighboring city to the southeast). Iglesia del Pueblo is predominantly Hispanic, though it has evolved into a multicultural congregation with a substantial number of Asian Americans, African Americans, Native Americans, and Euro Americans. José's pastoral focus is on youth and young adult ministries, teaching, and preaching.

A progressive urban ministry, Iglesia del Pueblo (translates to "Church of the People") is an active member of the Northwest Indiana Federation, an ecumenical organization of churches and mosques that addresses issues of justice in the northwest Indiana region in order to effect positive public policy and economic development. Currently, he serves as the Clergy Caucus chair of that organization.

José is passionate about addressing issues confronting youth and advocating for social justice. He plays a mean game of ping-pong, is a fan of the Chicago White Sox, and loves urban art and techno and hip-hop music. He is a club DJ part-time.

## Recommended Books, Web Sites, Blogs, and Other Resources

### *Theological Texts That Have Shaped (or Are Shaping) Me*

St. Augustine, *The Trinity* (New City Press, 1991).
Dietrich Bonhoeffer, *The Cost of Discipleship* (Touchstone, 1995).
Virgilio Elizondo, *Galilean Journey: The Mexican-American Promise* (Orbis, 2000).
Peter J. Gomes, *The Good Book: Reading the Bible with Mind and Heart* (HarperOne, 2002).
Stanley Grenz, *Theology for the Community of God* (Eerdmans, 2000).
Steven J. Land, *Pentecostal Spirituality: A Passion for the Kingdom* (Sheffield Academic Press, 1993).

### *Fiction and Creative Nonfiction That Have Shaped (or Are Shaping) Me*

Chinua Achebe, *Things Fall Apart* (Anchor, 1994).
Sherman Alexie, *Indian Killer* (Grove Press, 2008).
Jhumpa Lahiri, *The Namesake* (Mariner, 2004).
Chaim Potok, *The Chosen* (Ballantine, 1996).
Esmeralda Santiago, *When I Was Puerto Rican* (Da Capo Press, 2006).
Malcolm X, *The Autobiography of Malcolm X* (Ballantine, 1980).

## Favorite Quotes

I have come that they might have life, and that they might have it more abundantly.

—Jesus of Nazareth

Injustice anywhere is a threat to justice everywhere.

—Martin Luther King Jr.

God is of no importance, unless He is of supreme importance.

—Rabbi Abraham Joshua Heschel

Hope has two beautiful daughters. Their names are anger and courage: anger at the way things are and courage to see that they do not remain the way they are.

—St. Augustine

## Five Things to Do to Make the World a Better Place

1. To Americans: Become aware of our privilege and our abuse of that privilege in the world; sacrifice comfort.
2. To my peoples of color: The race struggle is not over just because you got a house in the suburbs; and to whites: Your guilt is not getting us anywhere; repent and reconcile.
3. To consumers: Refuse to accept society's proclamation that we are what we have; embrace simplicity.
4. To church people: Be intentional about your relationship with God and the radical things that that relationship calls for; practice the disciplines.
5. To so-called straight people: If Jesus were here today, he would chill with "the gays," so I encourage you to chill with Jesus for once; stand in solidarity.

## Contributor: Joshua Einsohn

Professional title: Casting Director and Marriage Equality Activist

Personal Web site: http://www.ALLorNotAtAll.org

Bio: I was born and raised in Dallas, where I attended St. Mark's School of Texas for twelve years . . . then off to college at Washington University in St. Louis . . . and since then, I've worked in the entertainment industry in Los Angeles for about fifteen years, which is usually less impressive than it sounds.

When Proposition 8 passed in California and my right to get married was taken away, I also became an activist . . . a true case of "You don't know what you've got 'til it's gone."

## Recommended Books, Web Sites, Blogs, and Other Resources

Karen Rauch Carter, *Move Your Stuff, Change Your Life* (Fireside, 2000).
Benjamin Hoff, *The Tao of Pooh* (Mandarine Books, 1992).
Harold S. Kushner, *When Bad Things Happen to Good People* (Anchor, 2004).

## Favorite Quotes

All the beautiful sentiments in the world weigh less than a single lovely action.

—James Russell Lowell

Be humble, for you are made of dung. Be noble, for you are made of stars.

—Serbian proverb

## Five Things to Do to Make the World a Better Place

1. Adopt a pet from a rescue organization. It's possible to get purebred animals without going to a breeder . . . I did!
2. Go outside your comfort zone and attend another religion's services or volunteer for an organization that is in your community but serves people who are different from you.
3. Be nice! When you take out your temporary anger or frustration on some hapless bystander, you've ruined part of their day, too. Who exactly did that help?
4. Take a breath and ask yourself how your decisions will affect other people before you make the decision.
5. You know what you do well: cooking or talking or writing or shopping or gardening or whatever. Find someone who needs your skill set and volunteer to share it with an organization that could use the help. And spend some time looking for a small, local group that doesn't have access to the resources of the huge aid organizations.

## Contributor: Joshua A. Toulouse

Professional title: Youth Minister, Central Christian Church, Weatherford, Tex.
Personal blog and podcast: http://retrospectivereflections.blogspot.com; http://thegeniusthatis.podbean.com

Bio: Joshua is a seminary student at Brite Divinity School in Fort Worth, Texas, working on his Master of Divinity. He hopes to continue on for his Ph.D. and plans to become a college professor. In the meantime, he enjoys working with middle school and high school youth.

### Recommended Books, Web Sites, Blogs, and Other Resources

Textweek: http://www.textweek.com/movies/themeindex.htm. This is an awesome site that has many themes listed that you can click for movies that illustrate them.

### Favorite Quote

In the beginning the Universe was created. This has made a lot of people very angry and has been widely regarded as a bad move.
—Douglas Adams

### Five Things to Do to Make the World a Better Place

1. Practice what you preach. Stop the hypocrisy; truly act the way that we all say that we should instead of just paying it lip service.
2. Smile more. Seems like it's easy, but I really think that it would make a big difference if we all truly had a more positive attitude. Too often, we let the world drag us down.
3. Volunteer. Give of yourself one day a month. If everyone did this, we would accomplish more then we can imagine.
4. Pray. Prayer works, but I don't think that even believers do it enough.
5. Find something you are good at and do it. The world would be a better place if we all found a way to practice our hobbies, or ideally worked in a field that we love.

## Contributor: Kathy Escobar

Professional title: Co-Pastor
Personal Web sites and e-mail: http://www.kathyescobar.com; kathy@therefugeonline.org: http://www.therefugeonline.org

Bio: Kathy Escobar, M.A., co-pastors The Refuge, an eclectic faith community in north Denver dedicated to those on the margins of life and faith. She blogs on faith, life, and church at http://www.kathyescobar.com and is a founder and cultivator of Voca Femina, a creative arts site for women.

Deeply dedicated to helping individuals and groups explore a raw, authentic faith journey, she has coauthored two books on spiritual direction: *Come with Me: An Invitation to Break Through the Walls between You and God* (*Discovery House, 2002*), and *Refresh: Sharing Stories, Sharing Faith (New Hope Publishers, 2007)*. She lives in Arvada, Colorado, with her husband and five children.

## Recommended Books, Web Sites, Blogs, and Other Resources

Center for Transforming Ministry: http://www.ctm.org.
Henry Cloud, *Changes That Heal* (Zondervan, 1997).
Bruce Demarest, *Satisfy Your Soul* (NavPress, 1999).
Danielle Shroyer, *The Boundary-Breaking God* (Jossey-Bass, 2009).
Jean Vanier, *Community and Growth* (Paulist Press, 1989).

## Favorite Quotes

If you can't feed 100 people, just feed one.

—Mother Teresa

Blessed are the poor in spirit . . .

—Jesus

Get ready. God is preparing you for something really, really small . . .
—Shane Claiborne

Hope begins in the dark. The stubborn hope that if you just show up and try to do the right thing, the dawn will come. You wait and watch and work. You don't give up.

—Anne Lamott

If I can stop one heart from breaking I shall not live in vain; If I can ease one life the aching, or cool one pain, or help one fainting robin into his nest again, I shall not live in vain.

—Emily Dickinson

## Five Things to Do to Make the World a Better Place

1. If you engage in a conversation with a hurting person, follow up with them on it. Most people don't. Run toward the pain, pray for them, check in with them, and let them know you are thinking of them and they aren't alone.
2. If you can, buy a gift card or an extra bag of groceries every time you are at the store and pass it on to someone who might need it. You don't have to make a big deal of it, just slip it to them, or get it in the hands of someone who will know someone who is struggling.
3. Make yourself invite a neighbor or someone you normally don't hang out with for dinner.
4. Go hang out at your local social services/food stamp/Medicaid office for a few hours and learn what life is like for them. Just observe. Notice the shame. Notice the pain. Ask God to show you what you are supposed to do about it.
5. Bring a bunch of bus tokens to your local women's shelter. They always need them.

## Contributor: Marcia Ford

Professional title: Author and editor
Personal Web site: http://www.marciaford.com
Bio: Marcia Ford is the author of twenty-five books you've never heard of. But that's OK, because she's content to live in obscurity as long as she can do so in the Colorado Rockies. She writes, edits, knits, and lives a good life in full view of Pikes Peak's North Slope.

## Recommended Books, Web Sites, Blogs, and Other Resources

Leif Enger, *Peace Like a River* (Atlantic Monthly Press, 2002).
Everything C. S. Lewis ever wrote.

## Favorite Quotes

Do the right thing. It will gratify some people and astonish the rest.
—Mark Twain

When I stand before God at the end of my life, I would hope that I would not have a single bit of talent left and could say, "I used everything you gave me."
—Erma Bombeck

### Five Things to Do to Make the World a Better Place

1. Smile at strangers, especially those who don't look like you.
2. Volunteer your time somewhere outside your comfort zone.
3. Treat your family with the same courtesy you extend to others.
4. Slow down.
5. Be kind to someone who doesn't deserve your kindness.

## Contributor: Nadia Bolz-Weber

Professional title: Pastor

Personal Web site, blog, and e-mail: http://www.sarcasticlutheran.com; http://www.houseforall.org; sarcasticlutheran@gmail.com

Bio: Nadia Bolz-Weber is a very lucky gal; she gets to be the pastor of House for All Sinners and Saints in Denver, Colorado, a Lutheran emerging church. She is the author of *Salvation on the Small Screen? 24 Hours of Christian Television* (Seabury, 2008) and of *The Sarcastic Lutheran* blog.

Nobody really believes she's an ordained pastor in the ELCA (Evangelical Lutheran Church of America). Maybe it's the sleeve tattoos or that she swears like a truck driver. Either way . . . she's fine with it. Nadia lives in Denver with her family of four where she can be found writing bios in the third person and chasing chickens around the backyard with her kids.

### Favorite Quotes

The church is a bitch and a whore and the mother of us all.
—Martin Luther

Remove from Christianity its ability to shock and it is altogether destroyed. It then becomes a tiny superficial thing, capable neither of inflicting deep wounds nor of healing them.
—Søren Kierkegaard

Is it possible, I wonder, to say that it is only when you hear the gospel as a wild and marvelous joke that you really hear it at all? Heard as anything else, the gospel is the church's thing, the pastor's thing, the lecturer's thing. Heard as a joke—high and unbidden and ringing with laughter—it can only be God's thing.
—Frederick Buechner

## Five Things to Do to Make the World a Better Place

1. Have humility.
2. Be unapologetic for who you are.
3. See Christ in others, especially the ones you don't like.
4. Be Christ to others, especially the ones you don't like.
5. Give more money away.

## Contributor: Rebecca Bowman Woods

Professional title: Writer/Editor

Personal Web site: http://www.rebeccabowmanwoods.com

Bio: Rebecca Bowman Woods believes that everyone has a tale worth telling. She earned a Master of Divinity degree from United Theological Seminary in Dayton, Ohio, in 2006, with a concentration in digital culture ministry, and is an ordained minister in the Christian Church (Disciples of Christ). She was the news editor and director of digital media for *DisciplesWorld* magazine until it closed at the end of 2009.

Her work has appeared in *Just Women, United Church News,* the *New Catholic Encyclopedia* (2010 Supplement), and the *Fellowship of Prayer Lenten Devotional* (Chalice Press, 2008). She is the producer/director of *Beyond Borders: Faith and Action in the Arizona Desert* (2007), a thirty-minute documentary about the work of faith-based groups along the Arizona-Mexico border. Rebecca works as a freelance writer, editor, and media creator, occasionally preaching and speaking in the Cincinnati area. She and her husband, Dan, have four children.

### Recommended Books, Web Sites, Blogs, and Other Resources

Marcus J. Borg, *Reading the Bible again for the First Time: Taking the Bible Seriously but Not Literally* (HarperCollins, 2001).

Michael Joseph Brown, *What They Don't Tell You: A Survivor's Guide to Biblical Studies* (Westminster John Knox Press, 2000).

Liz Curtis Higgs, *Bad Girls of the Bible* (Book, DVD, Study Guide; I prefer the DVD). Those who enjoy *Bad Girls* will want to check out *Really Bad Girls, Slightly Bad Girls,* and Higgs's most recent, *Unveiling Mary Magdalene.*

Lisa Wolfe, *Uppity Women of the Bible* (Four DVD set, available at http://www.livingthequestions.com).

Heidi Bright Parales, *Hidden Voices: Biblical Women and Our Christian Heritage* (Smyth & Helwys, 1998).

### Favorite Quote

Everywhere is somewhere. Everybody's somebody's child.
—Singer/songwriter Tim Easton

### Five Things to Do to Make the World a Better Place

1. Smile. Mother Teresa once said, "Every time you smile at someone, it is an action of love, a gift to that person, a beautiful thing." It's the simplest way to acknowledge that we are all God's children.
2. Learn a language other than English. Many people in our communities are isolated by a language barrier. Language is humanity's way of bringing order to the chaos. If you read the creation story in Genesis 1, you'll notice that naming—giving words to something—is part of God's act of creating. Instead of always expecting other people to cross the barriers of language and culture, why not be willing to take a step into their world?
3. Become familiar with the systems and resources in place in your community. As Christians, we can always offer to pray for those in need. But if we are familiar with the systems and resources in our community, we can also point people in the direction of practical, tangible help. Sometimes churches start a program or ministry to meet a need, but other times, we can find God already at work and affirm these efforts.
4. Bridge the generation gaps. Western culture is age-centric. Young people spend their time with young people doing the things young people do; old people do the same. We miss so many opportunities to learn and be inspired by each other. Be willing to seek out those who are much younger or older than you are, and build relationships.
5. Grow something. A garden is a wonderful place to be constantly reminded of the still-unfolding miracle of creation. If you don't have space for a garden (or the energy to deal with the upkeep), even a single potted marigold will do. Growing things keep us connected to the earth and the beautiful mystery of life.

# God Image Survey

Researchers from Baylor found that by determining more about people's perceptions of God, they could predict much more about their moral and political beliefs than by looking at their faith background. The survey asked questions about participants' understanding of God, and from this they developed a formula for determining where their God image fell along a two-dimensional spectrum. The two dimensions include the following:

God's level of engagement—the extent to which individuals believe that God is directly involved in worldly and personal affairs.

God's level of anger—the extent to which individuals believe that God is angered by human sins and tends toward punitive, severe, and wrathful characteristics.

From the results, they came up with four general "God Image" types:

- Type A—Authoritarian: God has both a high level of engagement and a high level of anger.
- Type B—Benevolent: God has a high level of engagement and a low level of anger.
- Type C—Critical: God has a low level of engagement and a high level of anger.
- Type D—Distant: God has a low level of engagement and a low level of anger.

In the workshops that I facilitate around the country, I have found that people have a hard time talking about God sometimes. Often, either the conversation remains superficial and abstract or it dissolves into ideological argument. With this God Image tool, however, I have found that people can speak in a more narrative style about where their images of God come from and how this informs their faith. In doing this, we become storytellers rather than preachers or judges of one another, and we learn from one another's imaginings of the divine.

I asked each contributor to this book to take the God Image survey so that you could catch a glimpse into how each imagines God. I also included the survey in the book so that you and your friends or family can also take it and, hopefully, talk about your results.

How do you match up with our contributors? Does how they imagine God seem to affect their answers? How about you? Do you find you agree more with those who share a more common image of God? Did the survey results surprise you?

## God Image Survey

Remember, there's no right or wrong answer. Consider this a tool, a stepping-off point into deeper, more meaningful reflection, dialogue, and inquiry.

Based on your personal understanding, what do you think God is like? (Please mark only one.)

1. A cosmic force in the universe

   Agree          Disagree

2. Indifferent

   Agree          Disagree

3. Formless

   Agree          Disagree

4. Angered by the state of the world

   Agree          Disagree

5. Concerned with my personal well-being

   Agree          Disagree

6. Displeased by human sin

   Agree          Disagree

7. Will pass judgment after we die, but not before

   Agree          Disagree

8. Has had little or nothing to do with the world since it began

   Agree          Disagree

9. Cares about human suffering but doesn't interfere

   Agree          Disagree

10. Pure energy

    Agree          Disagree

11. All-powerful

    Agree          Disagree

12. Allows us to stray

    Agree          Disagree

13. Has no human characteristics or emotions

   Agree          Disagree

14. Analytical

   Agree          Disagree

15. Concerned but removed from worldly affairs

   Agree          Disagree

16. Forgiving

   Agree          Disagree

17. Friendly

   Agree          Disagree

18. Disappointed by humanity's treatment of one another

   Agree          Disagree

19. Wrathful

   Agree          Disagree

20. Kingly

   Agree          Disagree

21. Loving

   Agree          Disagree

22. Motherly

   Agree          Disagree

23. Punishing

   Agree          Disagree

24. Yielding

   Agree          Disagree

## Scoring Key

The questions are divided into four types: A, B, C, and D. Each question marked with "agree" is worth one point. "Disagree" is worth zero. To find out your score for each type, add up the number of "agree" responses for each question grouped below.

Circle the following questions you marked as "agree":

| | | | | | | |
|---|---|---|---|---|---|---|
| 4 | 6 | 11 | 20 | 23 | 19 | (The total number circled is your "A" score) |
| 5 | 16 | 17 | 21 | 22 | 24 | (The total number circled is your "B" score) |
| 7 | 9 | 12 | 14 | 15 | 18 | (The total number circled is your "C" score) |
| 1 | 2 | 3 | 8 | 10 | 13 | (The total number circled is your "D" score) |

Plot your results on the graph below:

| | | | | |
|---|---|---|---|---|
| 6 | | | | |
| 5 | | | | |
| 4 | | | | |
| 3 | | | | |
| 2 | | | | |
| 1 | | | | |
| | A | B | C | D |

## God Image Results for Contributors

Here's a breakdown of how our esteemed contributors fared on our God Image survey. See who you're most like and whose God Images surprise you.

### Becky Garrison

Authoritarian (6)
Benevolent (6)
Critical (2)
Distant (1)

### Brandon Gilvin

Benevolent (6)
Critical (4)
Distant (3)
Authoritarian (2)

## Christian Piatt

Distant (4)
Benevolent (4)
Critical (2)
Authoritarian (1)

## Craig Detweiler

Benevolent (6)
Authoritarian (4)
Critical (4)
Distant (2)

## David J. Lose

Benevolent (6)
Critical (2)
Authoritarian (2)
Distant (0)

## Gary Peluso-Verdend

Benevolent (6)
Authoritarian (3)
Critical (3)
Distant (3)

## Jarrod McKenna*

Benevolent (6)
Authoritarian (4)
Critical (3)
Distant (3)

## Jason Boyett

Benevolent (6)
Critical (5)
Distant (4)
Authoritarian (3)

## Jim L. Robinson

Benevolent (6)
Authoritarian (5)
Critical (4)
Distant (2)

## José F. Morales Jr.

Benevolent (5)
Authoritarian (4)
Critical (2)
Distant (2)

## Joshua Einsohn

Distant (3)
Critical (1)
Benevolent (0)
Authoritarian (0)

## Joshua Toulouse

Benevolent (5)
Critical (2)
Distant (2)
Authoritarian (2)

---

* Jarrod desired to set alight the survey in a Molotov cocktail to be lobbed in frustration at the idols of false 2-D dichotomies that seek to box the mystery of the triune God into beliefs to be analyzed rather than life-rupturing events to be undergone. This arson was an act of worship.

## Kathy Escobar

Benevolent (6)
Critical (4)
Authoritarian (4)
Distant (1)

## Marcia Ford

Benevolent (6)
Authoritarian (4)
Critical (3)
Distant (3)

## Nadia Bolz-Weber

Benevolent (6)
Critical (4)
Distant (1)
Authoritarian (1)

## Rebecca Bowman Woods

Benevolent (6)
Critical (3)
Distant (3)
Authoritarian (3)